Knowing Yourself
Knowing God

Dr. John Shackelford

DEDICATION

To those who become weary of ego strivings,
may you find your True Self
in God.

Acknowledgments

I want to thank my writers' group with whom I have met every two weeks over the last three years. Without their encouragement and deadlines, I probably wouldn't have finished the book. A special thanks to Janna Hughes who has led our chapter of the North Texas Christian Writers' Group. Janna has critiqued my drafts, suggested better ways, and always encouraged me to keep writing.

Final technical editing was provided by Paul G. Smith of A.G. Publishing. Paul gave me much needed guidance on my first book. A writer/editor friend from church, Karin Anderson, provided a detailed grammar edit, and lots of encouragement that I had some good content to share.

I also want to give a special thanks to some folks who read my first manuscript in its entirety and gave me encouragement and some great feedback: Meredith Deemer, Colleen Herring, Mike O'Donnell, and Ruth Lindsay.

I appreciate my fellow pursuit group friends, David Nicholson and David Harris, who have patiently listened to me and encouraged me as I wrestled with my writings.

Thanks also goes to the love of my life, Lalla, who loves me and understands my desire to produce something of value. She has been a great model of pursuing God. She also has a gift for editing.

The *Knowing God* part of my book was heavily influenced by my pastor, Chip Bell, and his teachings since he returned from a life-changing sabbatical. I'm thankful for Chip's excellent teachings on God's desire and God's sovereignty. God has gifted him with the desire and intellect to study and teach the complex truths of the Bible. Chip has constantly challenged me to rethink my concept of God.

I also appreciate my six friends from church who bravely shared their stories of pursuing Jesus.

Book cover design was the creative work of Anthony Carrillo. The Grand Canyon image Anthony chose conveys a sense of depth, beauty, and grandness, appropriate to the journey of knowing oneself and knowing God. It was a pleasure to work with Anthony.

Finally, I want to thank my Friday morning breakfast friend of the last fifteen years, Mitch Vaughn. God knew what He was doing when he arranged for us to be friends. Being an electrical engineer and a technology guy, Mitch has advised me on my building projects, wired my treehouse, and formatted my book for publishing. He has always been a willing consultant, encourager, and friend.

Contents

Contents

Introduction

College psychology opened a door. I peeked in and acquired some head knowledge. But in graduate school, founded by Christian psychologists, I walked through the door and began living there. My classmates lived there too. We not only read the psychology, we applied it to our lives. We also integrated it under the truth of our Christian faith. And we began to know ourselves. Only began.

You may seek to know and understand yourself too. To that end, I've packed thirty years of experience into this book. More than just read the words, I hope you enter a life-stage of accelerated self-discovery. I hope you will live it and breathe it. Read each chapter and discuss it with a close friend. I will show you some helpful personality models. Take a look. Try some on. See what fits. You will recognize your type, your temperament. Also, I want you to know your feelings. I want you to face and begin to work through old hurts. Discover the deepest, truest you.

I have divided the book into three parts that will help you understand and process what it means to know yourself and what it means to know God.

Part I: Knowing Yourself

- Personality Type. Here you will meet people who are like you and people who are quite different. You will become more aware of how you are wired and what motivates you. There will be stories. While no two people are exactly alike, people do fall into types that give a framework for understanding. As you gain insight into how people are different, you become better able to get along and appreciate them. I will present two personality type systems. Each system has a test you can take.

- Personal History, Healthy and Unhealthy. In this module you can find a description of a healthy family atmosphere which helps children develop into secure individuals, free to develop according to their unique design. There is also a contrasting description of the unhealthy family system. Children of this system develop negative coping strategies, which take them away from their original bent. They grow up with confusion about who they are. They're too busy striving to feel secure to know who they are. Seeing these two paths of development, may help you see what you missed in childhood, and provide insight into your particular coping strategies. These strategies helped you survive childhood but limit you as an adult. The coping may keep the truer you from developing. Recognizing and dealing with what has happened to you is a huge part of knowing yourself. If you are a parent, this material helps you know how to raise an emotionally healthy child.

Part II: Knowing God

One of the foundational tools for knowing ourselves is to know the God who designed and created us in His image. To know God better, we will look at His gift, His will, and His desire. I believe as you draw close to Him, He will reveal more about Himself and more about you.

Part III: The Stories

The final part of this book is real life examples of Christians seeking a deep relationship with God. Here you will find six stories of Christians who have desired to know God better. They share how God has loved them and changed them. Most also share how they have come to know themselves better in the process.

Excerpts (shaded) from the stories in Part III are placed strategically throughout the book to illustrate points of a particular chapter.

Come with Me

Come along on this journey to know yourself. Perhaps you will identify with some of my misguided attempts to develop and achieve. Looking back, these were necessary steps to know myself and to know God better. Mentors and friends have helped me immensely along the way. I again encourage you to read this book with a friend or small group with whom you can discuss and apply these concepts. I wish I had read a book like this when I was thirty. Let me help you know yourself. Let me encourage you know God in a more intimate way.

Part I: Knowing Yourself

Chapter 1

Beginning To Know My Feelings

Our Adventure
March 15, 1973

As usual, I skipped lunch and played an hour of full-court basketball with some of the staff at Methodist Children's Home. Returning to my '63 Chevy, I noticed a white envelope on the car seat. My wife, Lalla, must have dropped it off, knowing I would want to see this right away. The return address said Rosemead School of Psychology. I had applied to their Ph.D. program in counseling psychology. It was hard to get into a Ph.D. program in psychology. I had already been accepted at The University of North Carolina to get a master's degree in social work. I tore open the crisp envelope and read, "John Shackelford, we are pleased to inform you've been accepted into the 1973 Class of Rosemead School of Psychology".

Stunned, it took a minute for my shock to turn to excitement. I knew I had a big decision to make. Do I take the safe road and go to a proven, well-respected program at the University of North Carolina, or do I take a risk on this upstart school in California? This new school, Rosemead, had great appeal because of their stated mission of integrating psychology and theology. But Rosemead was only two years old and still in the process of accreditation. Also, I didn't know much about where they were coming from spiritually. I didn't want to move out there only to discover their view of Christian counseling was offering spiritual clichés like, "Just trust God."

A couple of weeks later I took a red-eye flight to Southern California to check out the school. It was my first time to fly on a commercial airliner. The jet seemed like a time machine, converting twenty-five hours of driving to three hours. I arrived just before dawn, rented a compact car, and drove through the heaviest traffic I had ever seen. Daylight tried to come from the east, but it was dull and muted. I concluded it was a foggy day, but I soon learned it was the famous Los Angeles smog.

At the school, I met Dr. Richard Mohline, dean of students, who warmly talked with me and showed me around. I met another professor and some students. I could see their excitement about integrating psychology and theology. They were very nice, and there was no weird spiritual vibe. I flew back the next night, sharing my excitement with my wife at 3:30 am.

Being rather obsessive and perfectionistic, I hated the thought of making a big mistake. After seeking God's guidance as best I could, we decided to go to Rosemead. It felt like a step of faith, but God helped me realize that if it didn't turn out to be the sound psychology training I wanted, I could probably still go to a good school of social work.

I must explain that in 1973 some Evangelicals (Christian churches which emphasize the authority of the scriptures) thought psychology was at least suspect, and more likely "a tool of the devil." But I believed studying psychology would better equip me to help Christians who were hurting. Unconsciously, I probably hoped I would find help for myself.

One hot August day, we left Waco, Texas and struck out for California, quite an adventure for two small-town kids. With an orange U-Haul trailer behind each car, we crossed the Great Southwest, stopping to enjoy the view of the Grand Canyon along the way. What an adventure! I was twenty-four and Lalla was twenty-two. My mother didn't understand why we had to go to a school in California. "It's so far away, and they have earthquakes, you know," she warned. She certainly didn't understand this "psychology" I wanted to study.

At Rosemead, I met other couples and individuals who had come to study psychology and theology. My professors explained that "all truth is God's truth," whether it is discovered by Dr. Sigmund Freud or Sir Isaac Newton. Rosemead encouraged students to grow emotionally, as well as to learn the psychological material. Students were each required to be in group therapy for a year and individual therapy for one to two years.

By nature and nurture, I am a shy and inhibited person, fearful of making mistakes and fearful of offending anyone. I had never really been "in touch" with my feelings. I wanted to please people and achieve in whatever I did. Emotionally, I was pretty shut down. That was about to change.

My Secret Exposed

During the spring of my first year, during a group experience with fellow students, I shared my dark secret. There were ten of us sitting in a circle. The exercise instructed us to anonymously write something on a piece of paper that had been hard or painful in our past. We then folded the paper and put the papers in the middle of the circle. We were to each draw a paper and do our best to empathize with what the person had shared. I don't even remember which classmate read my secret. But they tried to empathize and then they began to discuss it. I was so anxious and guilty; I interrupted and told them it was me. Looking back, it is amazing what I wrote on my piece of paper: "When I was nine, I was in a homosexual relationship for two years."

When they found out the relationship was with a twenty-four-year-old man in my church, one of the guys compassionately said, "John, that wasn't your fault. That was child abuse." I had carried so much shame and fear for fifteen years. I felt like a prisoner hearing for the first time that I might be pardoned. The others guys agreed and gave me a lot of support for taking the risk of sharing such a big thing. I don't think I was that brave. I just desperately needed understanding and forgiveness. I was tired of hiding and fearing someone would find out.

Another student asked me if I had told my wife about this. I said, "No, I've never told Lalla. What would she think of me?" He encouraged me to tell her. "I think she'll understand," he said. I drove home that night and spilled it. She was understanding and supportive.

Wow, what a day! I felt I didn't have to hide anymore. I didn't have to keep the secret. And could it be true that it wasn't my fault? After all, I was just a kid. Thank God for people who can listen and understand and warmly extend God's love in person. I went from being stuck in shame and fear, to being in the healing process, dealing with my underlying feelings of anger and sadness.

Isn't it amazing how the mind of a child will make some abuse their fault? For fifteen years I felt the guilt of being in a "homosexual relationship". Until I could tell someone about it, I couldn't see the truth that I was a child who was abused.

Good Grief

One Sunday night during our second year, I watched a movie about a high school soccer player who fought cancer. When in remission, he played soccer. In the end, he died. When that movie was over, I began sobbing. I couldn't stop. Lalla was shocked to see me like this. It caught me totally by surprise, but I began to understand it clearly.

I had grown up on a small farm fifty miles south of Fort Worth, Texas. While my dad's day job was in the city, in the evenings and on weekends he enjoyed raising cattle and goats. He even bought me a horse when I was nine. I did a lot with my dad on the farm, tagging along and helping more as I got older.

Two weeks before my high school graduation, dad asked if I would help him load a steer he was taking to market. After we got it in the trailer, he drove off headed to the market in a nearby town. Ten minutes later we got a call that he "passed out" while driving. My mom, little sister, and I jumped in the car and rushed to where he ran off the road. His car had veered into a ditch. He had lost consciousness and fallen over to his right in the seat of his El Camino pickup. Dad's skin was ashen and he wasn't breathing. We assumed it was a massive heart attack. And just like that, he was taken from us.

The next morning, still in shock, I remembered when I was ten and playing out in a back yard at night with some boys. Two of the older boys ran along the yard holding a rope near the ground. I got tripped, and I never saw it coming. In one second, I'm standing up and playing. In the next second, I'm lying on the ground, trying to figure out what happened. That was how I felt that morning after my dad died. My whole world had changed.

I now felt I had to be the strong one for my two sisters and my mom.

"Now I am head of the family," I thought.

As a boy, I had hardly ever let myself cry, at least in front of anyone. Boys weren't supposed to cry, and as head of the family, I wasn't about to go weak now. My mom began setting my plate at Dad's place at the dinner table. I was just eighteen.

That's not all. Four years before the movie incident, one month after Lalla and I were married, her dad was murdered. Talk about shock. He had been my major Christian role model. He was a small town physician who had been shot by a patient.

I got the call from my mom. The hardest thing I have ever done in my life was to hang-up and turn and tell my bride that her dad had been shot and that he died. Tears still come to my eyes as I write this.

When this tragedy happened, Lalla was nineteen with seven younger siblings. I felt I had to be strong for her, for her mom, and for all the younger siblings. I had become close to her little brothers over the previous eight years. So I didn't let myself grieve that loss either. I just stuffed it all down and tried to "be strong." Now, with this sad movie, grief came gushing out – long overdue.

The Truth about Feelings

Feelings are "suspect" in Evangelical circles. Many believe feelings are fickle...feelings can't be trusted...feelings can get you in trouble." Some Christians would contrast the fickleness of feelings with the solidity of truth in the Bible. They presented it as an either/or situation. Either you trust your feelings or you trust God.

But it is not an either/or. God made us in His image with the capacity to feel as well as to think. In my story, by not recognizing my feelings and grieving, I was blocked from the healing I needed. The Bible says that Jesus was a man acquainted with grief. He grieved over the lost. He grieved when his friend Lazarus died. In many places, the Bible talks about God's feelings - love, delight, anger, etc.

Early family messages have a lot to do with this too. Parents sometimes allow certain feelings in their children and don't allow other feelings. In my family, it was okay to be scared, but sadness and anger - not so acceptable. My culture told me only babies cry. Strong boys don't cry.

As a psychologist, I learned that it is healthy to let myself grieve. Crying is a normal part of grief. Crying or talking about my sadness helps me move through the grief process. The sooner I go through the grief process, the sooner I am back to a normal or positive mood. If I don't face my grief, I get stuck in the sadness or anger. That can turn to depression.

A metaphor I will never forget came from one of my Rosemead professors, John Carter. He explained that repressing a feeling is like trying to hold a beach ball under water. You can only hold it there so long before your hands start shaking as they weaken under the building pressure. Suddenly the ball bursts up, out of control. That is what often happens with a hurt or an anger that we don't face. It pops up in some destructive or hurtful way. It doesn't magically go away. Feelings need to be respected and processed. There are two classic ways of coping when we don't acknowledge and process painful feelings: (1) We may "act out" feelings with rage or alcohol or drugs or sex, or (2) we may internalize or "stuff" painful feelings which can lead to clinical depression or an anxiety disorder.

Dashboard

Author Gordon MacDonald conveys the importance of feelings by using the illustration of a car's dashboard. We know how important it is to watch the gas level, the oil level, and the temperature. We "get it" that the instruments on the dash are giving us crucial information. This information keeps us functional and on the road. We can see when we need gas or water, and we stop and get what we need. We are not so adept at reading our feelings and our needs. (MacDonald, 1997, p. 83)

It's a challenge we all have – to be aware of our feelings and needs and deal with them. Being aware of our emotions and our needs can lead to us taking better care of ourselves and our loved ones. When we go for a long time ignoring our inner dashboard, we find ourselves "broken down" by the side of the road.

Conclusion: Being aware of our unpleasant feelings is part of knowing ourselves. Being aware of bad feelings helps us deal with these feelings. It could be anger. It could be hurt. It could be grief. The more we deal with our feelings, the less we get stuck in negative modes, and the less we make destructive decisions. As mentioned earlier, when we don't deal with our unpleasant feelings, we may seek to numb ourselves through addictions, or we may sink into clinical depression or an anxiety disorder. Back to the Big Picture:

Knowing Yourself Business Metaphor

Imagine this. You just bought a business in a nearby town. But part of the deal is you can never make an onsite visit. You have to run it from a distance. A little weird I know, but stay with me.

You also can never meet or talk with the employees. You send them some directions through e-mail or text, but you never talk with them or get to know them. You also don't have control of the hiring or firing. Some days new people show up and work. You are never quite sure who is there and what they are up to, but you are hoping the work gets done and you make enough money to support yourself. When they mess up, guess where the buck stops. Right, it stops with you.

I'll bet you are thinking, "I would never buy a business in which I couldn't know and talk with my employees. That's just stupid."

You want a business where you can be onsite. See what's going on. You want to get to know your people. You want to know their personalities, their gifts, their skill sets. You want to give them job descriptions and manage them because you want to be successful and effective and make a profit.

We face a similar problem as we pursue a productive and fulfilling life. To accomplish this we need to have an awareness of this "self." We are mysteriously made up of many unseen parts or characters. We need to know these parts: their motivations, their personalities, their abilities, their values. We need to manage all of this to have a productive and fulfilling life.

My Desire for You

My desire is that when you finish this book, you will be much more aware of your feelings, your thoughts, your personality, and your issues. If you don't know yourself, it's as if you are walking around with your eyes closed. You are moving through life, but you are bumping into lots of things. Sometimes you hurt yourself. Sometimes you hurt others. But if you become more aware, more awake, then you are more consciously living in the present and making better decisions.

And as a Christian, knowing yourself better means knowing your ego-run life better. That's a helpful awareness, since we have been called by God to follow Him. Our original design in His image is to have a God-led life. This leads to more peace and security. Paradoxically, following God also leads to a life of great adventure. We usually never know what God is going to bring into our lives. We get to be a part of what He is doing in the world. To the extent we muddle along blindly, real peace and true security elude us, and we miss the exciting adventure.

Excerpt from Claire's Story

Breakthrough

Early in 2011 Claire and a couple of friends decided to create a group called a Pursuit Group. They would meet every two weeks and share their journal entries on their conversations with God/Jesus. Within a few weeks the church had the annual Women's Retreat in East Texas. That Friday night one of her best friends mentioned something about the True Self. Claire said in an angry tone, "What does that even mean?" They talked. Her friend told her that there was something blocking her from talking and getting

---

close to God. There was a long, long silence. Finally Claire began to cry. "I wailed". Claire, with the accountant personality, was not one to get emotional, much less wail. Letting her pain out was long overdue. As she went to bed that night, she felt a little better – like a great burden had been lifted off her back.

By the next morning, the resentment was gone. Later that morning the speaker told the story of Jesus healing a woman bent over for eighteen years. Claire realized, "That's me." She began telling the other women what had happened. "I was so excited."

By the next Pursuit Group meeting, Claire had been spending time with God and journaling about it. It had been a very meaningful time and she felt Jesus was speaking to her. Not an audible voice of course, but a voice in her head that sounded more like Jesus than Claire.

Very soon after this Claire read the little book, *The Gift of Being Yourself*, by David G. Benner. It was about the True Self and Claire realized she needed to discover this True Self rather than trying to keep up a front and be the strong, competent person to all who needed her. (Benner D. G., 2004)

Claire's full story can be found in Part III: The Stories

Questions for Reflection

Identify a trauma or loss in your life.

- Did you grieve about it at the time? Did you grieve it sometime later?

- Did anyone really listen and help you through this experience? If so, who?

- How did that trauma or loss affect you or change you? Affect your thinking? Affect your behavior?

- If the trauma was the result of someone else's behavior, have you forgiven the person who hurt you?

- The psychologically healthy person can be aware of all their feelings, even unpleasant feelings: fear, hurt, anger, sadness, shame, and loneliness.

- Are there some feelings that you don't let yourself feel or have? Why? Explain.

- What can you do to learn to accept and value all your feelings? Feelings are important, but you are much more than your feelings. We process our feelings, so they won't control us or drive us to be destructive to ourselves or others.

Chapter 2

Getting To Know the Ego

We use the term ego in different ways. When we say someone has a big ego, we often mean they are full of themselves. If we say someone has a strong ego, we usually mean he is forceful about doing things his own way. Or we think of someone with a weak ego as lacking in confidence and self-esteem. But how has psychology defined the ego?

Sigmund Freud Identified the Ego

Freud viewed the baby as all Id. The Id contains the infant's raw, instinctual drives to get his needs met. The Id operates on the pleasure principle. When dirty and wet, baby cries. When hungry, baby screams. The Id does not care about the external world. It just wants what it wants. (Freud, The Ego and the Id (The Standard Edition of the Complete Psychological Works of Sigmund Freud, 1990)

The ego develops to mediate for the baby. The ego operates on the reality principle. Ego learns parents and caretakers have their own priorities. Ego's job is to mediate between the raw Id's aggressive ways and the external world (parent) that has the goodies. The ego mediates between the Id and reality, so the child's needs can be met.

As the child grows, his ego becomes more adept, more sophisticated. When my grandson was two, he said, "Me wants more cake." Three years later at five, he finishes his dinner and dessert, and then asks, "Mom, if I eat more vegetables, can I have another piece of cake?" His young ego knows the rules of his world, and he knows how to improve the odds to get what he wants.

It's Me

What I think of as me, is my ego. It is my conscious identity of who I am. I am a nice guy. I love my family. I try to help people. I like to watch football. I am dependable. I am honest. I am creative. I like to remodel and build. I'm a dreamer. This is how I see myself. For the most part, I'm okay with it. This is me.

The Ego Has Important Functions

The ego is a part of us. The goal is not to eliminate it, no more than we would try to eliminate our brain. The ego is watching out for us, helping us make it in this world. Here are some important functions of the ego:

- Reality testing
- Impulse control
- Regulation of feelings
- Judgment
- Good relationships
- Thought processes
- Defensive functioning

My Ego Is Committed to My Security

Now, under the surface, in my unconscious, I have old wounds, conflicts, and contradictions. But my ego usually keeps those things unconscious, so they don't disrupt me from functioning. In fact, my ego's priority is my security rather than my growth. It may steer me away from growth and getting to know myself better, because that would stir up some anxiety. I had some hurtful and scary experiences in childhood. My ego remembers and strategizes to steer me away from hurt and danger. The ego keeps doing this throughout my life – even in situations where there is no threat and danger. Here are a couple of examples:

Thomas

Thomas grew up with a critical, perfectionist father. Thomas avoided expression of his thoughts and feelings when he was around others. He would never think of taking leadership, because he believed he would set himself up for criticism. His ego steered him away from being criticized.

Marlene

Marlene had a very controlling, critical mother. She feared she would be a similar mom. Knowing how much her mom hurt her, she decided not to have children. Her ego is steering her way clear of being a controlling mom. Her ego is successfully protecting her, but at what cost? Her ego didn't tell her she could resolve the pain and be a good mom.

By these examples, we can see how the ego, in protecting us, also keeps us from growing and changing. In fact, the ego has a small army of ego defense mechanisms, to keep things from changing.

High-Functioning and Low-Functioning Egos

Some people have a high-functioning ego which we believe comes from optimal biology, good parenting, and a stable environment. Such a person has the ego resources or ego strength to handle family and work responsibilities without having a breakdown.

Some less fortunate people arrive at adulthood with a low-functioning ego. They may have compromised biology, a history of abuse or neglect, or they have grown up in a chaotic environment. They may become extremely stressed or symptomatic with the average demands of family and work. Obviously, these are the extremes of high and low ego functioning and most of us fall somewhere in between.

Jennifer

Jennifer is a 45-year-old teacher and mother. She grew up in a middle class home, and her parents provided a lot of security and love. Jennifer (healthier ego) functions at a high level. Not only does she do a good job as a teacher, she manages a home with her husband and two children. A key part of her success is knowing what she needs and knowing her limits. Her good judgment keeps her from taking on too much. She knows she needs time for herself and time for her key relationships. Sure, some days get too hectic, but those are the exception. She knows she needs to recuperate from a crazy, stressful day, and re-establish the balance of giving and taking.

Kevin

Kevin is driven. He did without in his childhood and now he (less healthy ego) wants to have it all. He works long hours, coaches his daughter's soccer team, and drinks too much at night to relieve the stress. He and his wife are like the proverbial ships that pass in the night. He thinks someday, when the kids are gone, they'll be able to kick back and enjoy each other the way they used to do. He wants his family to have the nice things he missed as a kid, so he charges things he can't afford. He has several high-interest credit cards with higher and higher balances. Lately, the stress is too much and he's starting to experience panic attacks. While it appears he is functioning at a high level, he is not taking care of himself, he is not taking care of his wife's emotional needs, and his financial stability is at risk because of his debt. The panic attacks suggest his ego is cracking. He is headed for a collapse of some kind.

In later chapters, we will look at child development and what helps the formation of a healthy ego or healthy self. Actually, according to Jung and modern day psychologists, the ego is a subset of the larger Self.

The Ego Is Only A Small Part of the Self

Carl Jung, a contemporary of Freud, proposed a model that gave space for the spiritual within the very structure of man. He allowed for and believed in the mystical, the spiritual, which was an important departure from Freud. Jung saw the ego as the conscious part of the total Self. He believed Self was the bigger structure, that held the conscious and the larger unconscious as well. Like an iceberg has the larger part underwater, Self has the larger, unconscious part below consciousness. (Benner D. , 2011)

The diagram below illustrates that we each have a Self made up of that which is conscious and that which is unconscious. The ego is in the upper part in the diagram which represents the ego's adapting and coping. In the lower part of the diagram, the unconscioius, are painful memories, feelings, and unacceptable drives and desires.

Also deeper within is a part I think of as the soul. The soul has been considered the spiritual or immaterial part of a person. This is where I visualize connecting with God. My soul connects with God. To be theologically correct it's where my soul connects/unites with the Holy Spirit. Another may experience it as their soul connecting with Jesus. Both would be accurate.

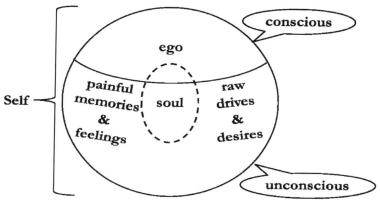

My diagram is intentionally simple, but for some it may be a beginning point in understanding how the ego and the total Self are related. (Various versions of Jung's more complex model can be found.)

Now, allow me to flesh this out with a story.

Personal Story: I've Got To Get Through that Entrance

Five years ago, at the farm where I grew up, I finished some carpentry work by noon, and needed to see a counseling client. I allowed fifteen minutes to get to my counseling office. I drove up the gravel road of our farm's entrance, which is bordered by rock walls. In the narrow driveway a huge flatbed truck parked, blocking my exit. The trucker was there to pick up a large bulldozer. I asked the driver why he was sitting there. He explained our entrance was a tight fit for the truck, and he was waiting for his boss to come and help. The boss would stop traffic, so the driver could back onto the road and get a straight shot at the driveway.

I felt frustrated because the truck blocked my route to my client. I didn't have my client's cell number to call and let her know I would be late. After pacing around a few minutes, I offered to stop the traffic myself, so he could get through the entrance. It took him a few tries, but he finally squeezed the truck through and out of my way. I drove out the entrance and raced to town. Arriving late at 1:15 pm, my client had already left. Once again I felt frustrated. I thought, "God, why did that truck have to be there, just at the wrong time?"

There's More Than One Way Off the Farm

Two days later, I felt amazed to recall there was another way off the farm! Before you think I'm totally stupid for not knowing that about my own farm, let me explain. Two weeks earlier, I'd hired bulldozing to clear some brush. The dozer driver needed matches to burn the piled up brush. In looking for a neighbor with matches, I discovered a dirt road that actually led from the back of our farm to a new housing addition.

So, just two weeks before I had driven off the farm on this little dirt road. Yet, under stress and time pressure to get to my client, I didn't remember this key bit of information, this new option.

This illustrates how under anxiety and stress, we don't really use our brains well. Instead, we regress to old solutions and old patterns of coping. When I saw my car was blocked by that truck, my anxiety went up and my ego started trying to figure out how to get through the gate. I had tunnel vision on getting that truck out of my way and getting to my client.

The Ego Is Limited

The question came to my mind, "Why didn't my ego remind me there was another way off the farm?" Obviously the information about the back road was recorded in my brain. For fifty-seven years of my life, there was only one way off the farm. I think my ego was freaking out right along with me. My ego (me) was trying to solve the problem of getting through the front entrance. My ego is not so good at applying new information. Under stress, I revert to my 1960 model ego with its limited coping strategies. At these times I'm operating on fifty year old software!

A protestant theologian, Langdon Gilkey, in writing about our ability to think openly and lovingly, noted this about the ego:

> But when man's self is basically threatened, when he is involved in a crisis, a new power enters the scene, a power seemingly stronger than either the moral consciousness or the objective mind. It is the embattled ego fighting with every weapon at its disposal for its own security.

Again, the ego under duress seeks to maintain security. I can only think about what I want and need right now.

Now, when my wife and I are confronted with a difficult problem which doesn't appear to be solvable, one of us will usually remind the other, "There's more than one way off the farm." It's a great metaphor for growth.

Let's Demote the Ego

Jung saw the first half of life as mostly about the development of the ego. At mid-life, the ego, under the stresses of life, often has a crisis and weakens. Jung believed a positive response to the ego crisis, is to undergo a re-organization of personality and goals. Hopefully, we realize there is something bigger and more important than the ego's individualistic strivings and solutions. Jung felt that those who did not accept and embrace this larger reality were prone to depression in the second half of life.

As St. Paul wrote in the letter to the Galatians: "It is no longer I who live, but Christ who lives in me." (Galatians 2:20) According to David Benner, "Paul tells us that his personality has been reorganized in such a way that it no longer revolves around his ego, but a larger center within himself that he calls the Christ within." Benner sees this transformational process as reassigning the ego from CEO to Vice President of Operations. Christ/God becomes the CEO. Christ leads. (Benner D. , 2011, p. 55)

Back to the Diagram

As we submit more of our ego thinking to God's thinking, I believe our soul, filled with Christ/Holy Spirit, expands. It takes over more of the ego and the unconscious. See expanded area of the soul.

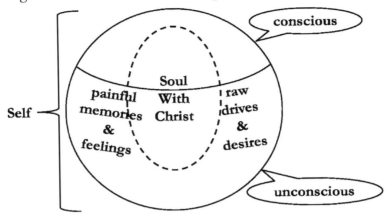

- I think our soul's expansion occurs at a conscious level as we study/ meditate upon the Scriptures, and as we get still and listen for God's leading (more on this in Part II – Knowing God)

- God does the major growth/transformation work deep inside us beyond our conscious knowing. Here are two relevant passages:

As the Spirit of the Lord works within us, we become more and more like him and reflect his glory even more. (2 Corinthians 3:18 NLT)

> Likewise the Spirit helps us in our weakness. For we do not know what to pray for as we ought, but the Spirit himself intercedes for us with groanings too deep for words. (Romans 8:26-27, ESV)

This is what I intended in my book's subtitle: Moving from An Ego-Led-Life to a God-Led-Life.

Hence, even our Christian growth is God's work, not our self-efforts. And it is going on deep inside us, orchestrated by God! A similar concept is the fruit of the Spirit. These are not qualities we strive for, but gifts from the Holy Spirit.

Metaphor for Growth

I would be remiss if I didn't state the obvious for emphasis. "There's more than one way off the farm" is a great metaphor for growth. Operating out of our ego, we are often rigid in the way we perceive life and the way we live life. We are often stuck or boxed in because we aren't aware that there are other options. From where we stand (in our ego) we can't see another way.

Thus we need help from something outside of our ego. It could be a friend, a therapist, the Bible, something we read, or God. At least one of these is necessary for change. Once we see "there is another way off the farm" we can, with courage, choose differently and act differently.

Summary

This concludes our introduction to the ego. Let me summarize what we know about ego:

- Ego mediates reality for the child. It's what I think of as me.

- Ego is all about my security – keeping down anxiety.

- Ego does have important functions.

- Ego is the conscious, smaller part of my larger Self.

- My larger Self also contains the unconscious and the soul which is my avenue, my connection, to God.

- My ego is limited. It's based on my early 1.0 software.

- As I respond to God and spend time with Him, my soul expands and, Christ-in-me grows, demoting ego to V.P.

See Appendix for seven aspects of Ego Functioning with examples.

Questions for Reflection and Discussion

- Think of something stressful to which you adapted, such as a difficult parent or a major loss. Did your adaption cause you to live life differently from that point on? How so?

- This is your ego at work, trying to protect you from similar hurts in the future. Is it limiting you now? How?

- Another way to look at this: Have you noticed you are running some outdated software? You respond in automatic ways, because that's the way you have always done things. Does any example come to mind?

- Do these old, familiar ways keep you from connecting with people? Do these old ways prevent you from knowing and developing your abilities and gifts?

Chapter 3

The Five Voices Inside
Your Head

We each have five ego states. They can sound like five voices in your head.

In chapter two, we learned how Freud and Jung saw the ego developing during our early years and providing necessary functions such as: accurate perception, judgment, emotional regulation, and logical thinking. We also saw how our ego is limited and is more about our security than about our growth.

A couple of generations after Freud and Jung, ways of looking at the ego expanded into subparts of the ego, better known as ego states.

Looking for a More Practical Approach

My graduate studies in Los Angeles grounded me in depth psychology and psychoanalytic technique. Armed with psychoanalytic theory and technique from Los Angeles, I moved to Dallas and began practice in the Bible Belt in 1979. However, there was a disconnect between my approach and what my clients were expecting in the way of practical help.

I searched for a senior psychologist who could help me offer more practical help to my clients. Someone directed me to the Dallas office of John Gladfelter, Ph.D. Dr. Gladfelter was a warm and personable man who enjoyed his work. He believed people could change and grow. He gave them a framework to understand themselves, and he offered them tools for change.

Dr. Gladfelter practiced from a Transactional Analysis perspective which was developed by Eric Berne, M.D. Trained to be a psychoanalyst, Dr. Berne broke from the rigidity of psychoanalysis and created a new approach, he called Transactional Analysis or TA. It became known as TA, for short. The beauty of TA is its simplicity. Yet, TA is profound. I found this approach positive, exciting, and practical. I decided to use it in my practice. I would study Berne's work, and get supervision from Dr. Gladfelter.

My clients didn't want to hear a lecture on all the theories of personality; they just wanted to understand themselves and to get help. With TA, I had a simple, yet accurate way to help people understand themselves. I had a practical tool to help them change.

What Is Transactional Analysis?

Transactional Analysis is a theory of personality that identifies five ego states within every person. Each ego state is a mode of operating. You will be in one of the five ego states when you are talking to someone or when you are talking to yourself.

The five ego states are:

Critical Parent

Nurturing Parent

Adult

Free Child

Adapted/Rebellious Child

Throughout the day or even every few minutes, we switch from one ego state to another. Clues to which ego state is operating can be heard in the words we use, and our tone of voice, and can be seen in our body language.

For example, a mom might say, with a stern voice and her hands on her hips,

"Brent, get off that video game now and clean your room."

Brent scowls back at her and says,

"That's not fair. I'm finishing my game first."

This illustrates a mother in her Critical Parent and her teenage boy in his Rebellious Child. When we talk from our Critical Parent, we often hook (pull up) a Rebellious Child response. That information becomes a tool for analyzing your verbal transactions. TA helps you become more self-aware so that you function from your Adult ego state, which is less judging and controlling. That creates constructive communication.

I believe as you become aware of TA's five ego states, you will recognize them in yourself and others, and know yourself better. TA has certainly helped me understand myself better.

Help for Me, Help for My Marriage

As I studied TA, I realized that at age thirty-one, I was living too much from one of those ego states – the Adapted Child. I was still trying to please others and avoid criticism. I wasn't thinking for myself (Adult ego state) and doing what I thought best. I was still trying to be a good boy. This was a life-changing insight for me.

This also had implications for my marriage. Here, I often operated from the Adapted Child position. My wife, big sister of seven younger siblings, often operated from her Critical Parent ego state. The Critical Parent has lots of "shoulds and rules." I began to see the dynamic of our transactions. TA, with its five ego states, provided a way to analyze our transactions – in a way that helped us see the pattern of our relationship.

I might start an interaction out of my Adapted Child state, that would push her into her Critical Parent ego state. Sometime I felt more secure giving her the responsibility for something rather than risk taking responsibility myself. At times, she might speak out of her Critical Parent about what I "should" have done. I reacted in my Adapted Child with shame or fear. Or I might slide into my Rebellious Child, another TA ego state, and become angry in a passive way. I pouted and grew quiet.

We did this for ten years of marriage. Resentment had built on both sides. TA gave me a tool to analyze our communications and know how to change them. I realized I needed to operate more from my Adult state. My wife recognized her Critical Parent and learned how to speak from her Adult ego state. We each began to know ourselves better. We began to see our ingrained relationship patterns. TA helped our relationship, so we no longer built resentments. We found a positive way to communicate. It was simple, yet a powerful tool for change.

Let's look at the five ego states within.

Your Critical Parent Ego State

Critical Parent
Nurturing Parent
Adult
Free Child
Adapted/Rebellious Child

Here's a quick way to recognize when you're defaulting to your Critical Parent ego state. You're thinking or talking in terms of "should" and "oughts."

Examples:

"You should always turn in your work on time."

"I believe one should take a bath every day."

"People should be on time."

"A healthy person should exercise several times a week."

On the *negative side*, your Critical Parent ego state can be controlling or perfectionistic:

"You didn't load the dishwasher right." (Implying you should have done it my way)

"You made four As and this B," said in a critical tone. (Implying you should have been perfect)

While making these comments, you show a critical tone and parental body language, such as finger pointing or hands on hips.

The *positive side* of the critical parent is having or expressing beliefs and values that protect you and help you live constructively.

Some examples of constructive values:

- I should limit junk food and eat what is healthy for me.

- I should treat people with respect.

- If I drink, I shouldn't drive.

- I shouldn't take office supplies from work home for personal use.

- As well as teaching and modeling Christian values at home, I should take my children to Sunday school.

- If I see a child being abused, I should try to stop it or report it.

- If a salesman or even a friend is trying to get me to buy something or do something with which I am not comfortable, I should say "No."

These are all positive values we have adopted to take care of ourselves and those we love. It is from the positive Critical Parent state that we have the strength to set boundaries, and it is where we house our beliefs and values.

The Ten Commandments could be viewed as positive Critical Parent statements. They are guidelines of how we should live so as to be moral and avoid creating suffering for ourselves and others. The first commandment also orients us to God rather than to our ego.

Parent Tapes

Some TA writers call these nurturing or critical ways of thinking and operating the Parent Tapes, because we learn these very early in life. We espouse a value or belief that our brains recorded from our parents. These Parent Tapes become so ingrained in us, we play them automatically. Think of the old cassette tape player. A button is pushed and the tape begins.

Examples:

"Get your homework done before you go to play."

"Watch your mouth."

"Oh, what a cute baby!" (Nurturing Parent)

"Do what I say, not what I do."

"If you ever expect to be good at that, you've got to put in the time."

"Don't make me turn this car around."

Your Nurturing Parent Ego State

Critical Parent
Nurturing Parent
Adult
Free Child
Adapted/Rebellious Child

In your Nurturing Parent, you speak kind, encouraging words:

"Thanks for helping me. You did a nice job."

"You are very creative."

Conversely, negative Nurturing Parent is someone who over-nurtures or does too much for someone who is old enough to care for themselves. I remember feeling irritated years ago by a woman who kept trying to serve me at dinner. She kept asking if I wanted this or that. I felt like saying, "Just leave me alone for a minute. Give it a rest." Her over-nurturing was hooking my Rebellious Child.

Your Adult Ego State

Critical Parent
Nurturing Parent
Adult
Free Child
Adapted/Rebellious Child

In your Adult ego state, you think, problem-solve, and use logic. The Adult ego state is the best for giving and receiving information. It is key to positive communication.

Examples of being in your Adult ego state are:

- Balancing your checkbook

- Studying for an exam

- Reading a news article

- Informing someone of an event coming to town

Another way to think of the Adult ego state is to view it as the manager of yourself. The Adult gathers information from the Parent ego states and the Child ego states and then makes a decision.

This Adult ego state is not to be equated with acting grown-up or mature. A five-year year old has an Adult ego state. Dr. Eric Berne called this "The Little Professor." It operates on limited experience, using intuition. A child's Adult ego state doesn't have as much experience as the Adult ego state of a thirty-five year old. Yet, a child's Adult ego state is in place, and it processes information.

When a parent says to a whiny four-year-old, "Use your words for what you want," they are teaching the child how to communicate out of the Adult state.

Let me offer two examples of how to "clean-up" communication, turning a Negative Critical Parent communication into an Adult Communication:

"Jordan, why are you always dawdling? Get dressed for school NOW," yelled mom.

A more positive message from the Adult is: "Jordan, finish dressing quickly because it's almost time to leave for school," she said firmly.

Or consider this communication from a husband to his wife:

"Kristen, where's the hot sauce? How am I going to have nachos if there's no hot sauce," husband yelled angrily, implying she should have bought more hot sauce.

Thinking before he yells, he cleans it up into a positive communication from his Adult:

"Kristen, there's no hot sauce in the fridge. Do we have another jar somewhere?," he asks calmly.

Your Free Child Ego State

Critical Parent
Nurturing Parent
Adult
Free Child
Adapted/Rebellious Child

Picture a carload of kids getting into a swimming pool on opening day. They whoop and holler and run for the water. Now picture a sad little boy sitting on his front steps looking like he just lost his best friend. His dog has run away. These are two snapshots of the Free Child. One is excited and the other is sad. In our Free Child ego state we have access to our feelings.

The Free Child is a natural part of us. Some TA writers even refer to the Free Child as the Natural Child. Have you ever noticed how readily a one or two-year old is in touch with her feelings? If happy or excited, she jumps around and squeals with delight. If sad, her little mouth turns down and the tears flow freely.

A little one is also in touch with his needs. He is hungry, and he cries. He is uncomfortably wet, and he cries. If a toddler needs a hug from mommy, he reaches up.

Efforts to meet our needs are built-in, instinctual. God has programmed us to try to get our needs met.

However, you may have learned to *not express your needs and feelings*. Growing up in your family, you may have learned that sometimes you got a negative response if you screamed out your feelings and needs. You learned it was better to keep your feelings and needs to yourself. This is especially true if your parents were sometimes harsh or critical. You may even have concluded that your feelings or needs were bad. You may have squelched your feelings and needs to an extreme, so much that you no longer have awareness of your feelings and needs. If you aren't aware of key feelings and needs, then you don't know yourself. Our goal here is for you to know yourself.

In Touch with Feelings and Needs

Going through the socialization process, you probably got a little confused. When was it okay to show your feelings and needs, and when was it not okay?

The answer lies in distinguishing between awareness and expression. Awareness is good. It is an internal observing of what you feel and need. Expression, on the other hand, is behavior. It is the job of your Critical Parent and Adult ego states to figure out what is appropriate behavior (expression) for a particular situation.

In psychotherapy, I encourage clients to look inside and see what their Free Child feels. Angry? Hurt? Sad? Scared? Lonely? The Adult part of you needs that information. Whenever you are unaware of needs and feelings, they have a way of popping out at the worst times. Remember, a function of your Adult ego state is to manage your life. The Adult state needs that data to try to get your needs met.

The Playful Child

When young, play is your fulltime job. There is something wrong if you can't play as an adult. If you don't let yourself play, chances are you have a strong Critical Parent message that says: be productive, work hard, be responsible, don't be childish, don't be immature. Allowing such Critical Parent message to run your life is a setup for bitterness and depression.

I enjoy giving "permission to play" a driven person. It's like giving permission to enjoy life. Part of being a healthy person is having a strong sense of gratitude. People who can't play, who are workaholic, don't feel much gratitude. We may even think it's God who is driving us so hard, but it's usually just our own harsh Critical Parent.

Your Adapted Child and Rebellious Child Ego State

Critical Parent
Nurturing Parent
Adult
Free Child
Adapted/Rebellious Child

The fifth and final ego state we need to understand is our Adapted/Rebellious child ego state. This is an ego state often activated when we are around authority. It could be a boss, or a teacher, or even our spouse or a friend.

Growing up, we have to learn that we can't always do what we want. We have to clean-up our room when we want to play. We have to go to school in the mornings and do our homework after school. Later, we have to get a job and go to work. This is the Adaptive Child. It's part of growing up. We have to set aside what we want to do and do what someone else says we should do.

The flip side of the Adapted Child is the Rebellious Child. While the Rebellious Child sounds so "rebellious," it is needed. It is our Rebellious Child who stands up and thinks or says, "I don't like this. I don't want to do what you're saying."

Now this may not go over too well with your dad or your teacher or your boss, but it depends on the context. The Rebellious Child stands up for the Free Child ego state if some authority is being too controlling or taking advantage of you. An important point is that the healthy person is aware of their Rebellious Child's feelings. Being aware doesn't mean you verbalize your anger or your refusal. Your Adult ego state gets involved and uses that information from the Rebellious Child to decide how you will actually proceed.

Let's illustrate this with a story. Tony does drafting for an architectural firm. His boss stops by his cubical at 4 p.m. and gives him a drafting project and says,

"Tony, I want this done today."

Tony's Adult ego state gives it a quick look and estimates it's a three-hour project. He usually gets off at 5 pm. He could work late until 6 pm, but he has his son's sports banquet at 7 pm with the family. Tony is angry his boss dumped this on him at the last minute.
Tony's has at least three options:

Tony could go with the Adapted Child ego state. He sits everything else aside and dives into the drafting project. At some point, he calls his wife and tells her that his boss is making him work late and to take the family to the sports banquet without him. He'll meet them there later when he's finished. While doing the project, he feels really guilty about not being there for his son, and he feels a growing resentment toward his boss.

Tony could go with the Rebellious Child ego state. He is so mad. He walks into his boss's office, almost yelling, "Why would you dump this on me at the last minute? Find someone else to work late." Upon arriving for work the next day, he learns his boss was written him up for unprofessional conduct.

Tony could go with the Adult ego state approach. He thinks this is unfair, and he is angry. However, he takes a few deep breaths and gets back in his Adult ego state. He thinks about possible solutions, since it's really important that he not miss his son's banquet. Tony decides to talk with his boss about options. "Mr. Smith, I'd really like to finish this project for you but my son's sports banquet is at 7 p.m. and I don't want to miss that. When do you need this finished? The boss says he must meet with the customer tomorrow at 9 a.m. Tony says, "I could do part of it now and then come in early and get it finished by 9 a.m." His boss agrees. "I wouldn't want you to miss your son's banquet," he says.

With this solution, negotiated by Tony's Adult ego state, Tony feels good. He will be there for his son, and he doesn't feel resentful toward his boss.

The Rebellious Child Matures

Early in life, your Rebellious Child may impulsively blurt out in protest. As you mature, feeling the Rebellious Child stirring is more a signal to your Adult ego state, as it was for Tony. Your Adult ego state is the problem solver. Your Rebellious Child thinks,

"I'm not standing for this."

At the same time, your healthy Critical Parent reminds you, "You shouldn't explode and say something you'll regret."

Then your Adult ego state, like an Internet search engine, comes online and starts objectively exploring solutions.

The old adage about counting to ten when you get angry is pretty good advice. You want to get out of your Rebellious Child ego state before you say or do something foolish. But remember, the Rebellious Child has given you crucial information that your Adult needs to respect and use.

When the Adaptive Child Over-Adapts

While we all have to adapt to get along, some of us take it to an extreme, usually to our own detriment. If you are always adapting, and your Rebellious Child seems to be locked away in some basement, three bad things can happen:

- You may eventually become clinically depressed. If you are always giving in and never standing up and expressing your feelings and needs, you don't get your needs met. Likely, resentment is building, but the overly adaptive person often avoids conflict and sees their anger as bad. Thus anger gets turned inward against the self. There is an old psychoanalytic saying: Depression is anger turned inward.

- A second possible effect of being overly adaptive is that you get sick a lot. You have stomach problems, tension headaches, or back pains. Adapting too much and not getting your needs met for years may even be a hidden culprit in heart disease or cancer.

- The third possibility of the overly-adaptive person is that at some point, they have all they can take, and they flip to their Rebellious Child and explode or walk out. They might walk out of a job or they might walk out of a marriage. They take it and take it and take it, and then suddenly they're done.

Projection

Projection is an ego defense mechanism where you project (think movie projector) something from inside you onto another (think movie screen). If I grew up with a harsh, judging parent, then those experiences were introjected, recorded in my Critical Parent ego state. In a sense, I expect others to be critical or judging of me.

For example, I arrive home after work and my wife asks,

"Did you pick up the cleaning?"

I respond rebelliously,

"Give me a break. I had a hard day."

Or maybe I respond adaptively,

"I'm sorry. I don't know how I could forget that."

Now assuming my wife wasn't being critical, she was just asking for information, then I have projected my Critical Parent onto her and responded either angrily, out of Rebellious Child, or with shame, out of Adapted Child. Hopefully, over time, I can realize I'm carrying that strong negative Critical Parent, and that I tend to project it onto others even when they are not being critical. If I become more aware of this tendency, I can avoid responding out of the Adapted/Rebellious Child.

It works the other way, too. When someone does speak to me from their Critical Parent, I may react (emotionally), and respond with either my Adapted Child or my Rebellious Child. But if I'm aware of my feelings, I don't have to respond that way. I can think a minute, then respond out of my Adult ego state.

For example, my boss in frustration says,

> "When are you ever going to get around to the Roberts account?" (implying I should have had it done already)

I can think, then calmly respond out of my Adult ego state,

> "I know you want that done, but I've had to finish earlier requests first. I will have time to do that tomorrow."

Contamination

The Adult ego state, the logical, objective, problem-solving state, can be contaminated to some degree. If you grew up in an ethnic group that hated another ethnic group, then your Critical Parent (beliefs) may contaminate your Adult. As you spout something derogatory, you think you are stating objective reality (Adult), but you are actually expressing a prejudice. Your Adult ego state is contaminated.

Another possibility is your Free Child can contaminate your Adult. If you were traumatized by a dog attack when you were young, your Adult (like the ego trying to help with security) may see every dog as a potential threat. Even when a friendly dog comes along, your anxiety goes up, and your Adult misperceives and you freak out.

The contamination of the Adult is consistent with my point at the end of the last chapter. The ego is limited. It is affected by earlier programming. When Eric Berne, the originator of Transactional Analysis, worked with people, part of his therapy was to decontaminate their Adult. He helped them see where their Parent or their Child had contaminated the Adult ego state.

Big Picture

I have presented another way to know yourself. Everyone has these five inner states. We've X-rayed what is going on behind our talk and our behavior. We now have a tool to analyze what is going on, and we have a model of healthy functioning in the Adult ego state. Greater awareness makes for more constructive communication and better decisions.

Further reading: *TA Today: An Introduction to Transactional Analysis* by Joines and Stewart.

Questions for Reflection and Discussion

- Which of the five ego states do you feel is dominant for you? Explain or illustrate.

- Do you get into the Critical Parent ego state a lot? Is your Critical Parent usually turned outward toward others or turned inward toward yourself? To help you answer this question, ask yourself: do you often try to direct or control others, or do you tend to be (Joines, 2012) hard on yourself?

- Is it okay to get into your Free Child ego state? Do you tend to be in touch with what you are feeling? With what you are needing?

- Do you tend to be more of a Adaptive Child or a Rebellious Child? Do you fall all over yourself trying to answer this question, or do you refuse to answer this question?

Chapter 4

Discovering Your Personality Type

Two years into my private practice, I wished for a new way of thinking about my clients. Something other than thinking of them as obsessive, histrionic, dependent, or paranoid. My earlier psychoanalytic training gave me a way to understand psychopathology, but no way to understand the normal personality differences.

Within months of my wish, my close friend from graduate school, Greg Crow, introduced me to the Myers-Briggs Type Indicator. I recall Greg saying, "I think you will really like this."

Greg was right. I became obsessed with the Myers-Briggs. I consumed any material I could find. Within a year, I began offering a Myers-Briggs workshop for anyone interested in knowing themselves better. I used it with all my new clients. It was especially helpful to those with marriage issues and those with career questions.

My desire is to help you know yourself better through this section on the Myers-Briggs.

Discovering Myself

To me, at age 34, this test was a life-changing discovery. I learned significantly more about how God had made me. I knew I was introverted, but I never really accepted it until I studied the Myers-Briggs. It helped me see my strengths and uniqueness of my introversion. I realized I was okay, even if I was rather quiet and socially awkward around new people. In fact, maybe I had strengths being this way. I started appreciating myself as I understood the introvert's gifts and strengths.

My second discovery from the Myers-Briggs: I was an intuitive. That meant I was a dreamer, living out there in the future, always thinking about the possibilities. I could actually be creative. Artistic endeavors and creativity were not really valued or encouraged in my rural home or school. What was valued was following the rules, obeying authority, and doing things the right way. Discovering I was intuitive opened a whole new door. I had permission to think outside the box. In fact could even create some new boxes – and who says boxes have to be square or rectangular?

I had wished for a test to help me understand my clients. With the Myers-Briggs, I now had that tool. What I didn't expect was how much it would help me understand myself, my wife, and my key relationships.

To my surprise, my wife and I tested to be almost exact opposites! Let me tell you, this explained so much of our conflicts and misunderstandings. Oh, we had many similar core values and similar interests, but personality wise, we differed on three of the four Myers-Briggs preferences. For those of you who know the Myers-Briggs, I am an INFP, and she is an ESFJ. Do you wonder what these letters mean?

The Four Preferences

The Myers-Briggs is based on four preferences. I think of these as preferences and tendencies we have from birth, although they may be shaped to a small degree by family and environment.

You prefer	Extraversion(E)	or	Introversion(I)
You prefer	Sensing(S)	or	Intuition(N)
You prefer	Feeling(F)	or	Thinking(T)
You prefer	Judging(J)	or	Perceiving(P)

Depending on how you score on the Myers-Briggs, you are one of sixteen personality types. For example, if you prefer Extraversion, Sensing, Feeling, and Judging, you are an ESFJ. If you prefer Introversion, Intuition, Thinking, and Judging, you are an INTJ. There are fourteen other interesting types.

Extraverts versus Introverts
How you get your energy

Extraverts are outgoing and talkative with new people. They get energized by being with people. They are verbally skilled and have a breadth of interests.	Introverts are quiet and slow to show what they are thinking or feeling. They get energized by one on one relationships or solitary activity. They have deep interests.

Sensing versus Intuitive
How you gather information

Sensing folks use five senses to take in the world. They are good with details, routine, and common sense. They live in the now.	Intuitive people are dreamers who see the possibilities and big picture. They are into ideas and the abstract. They live in future.

Feeling versus Thinking
How you make decisions or judgments

Feelers tend to make decisions more based on values and how a decision will affect others. They are sensitive, warm, and subjective.	Thinkers tend to make decisions based on logic and the facts and what is truth. They are cool, detached and see things as black and white.

Judging versus Perceiving
How you prefer to live life

Judging folks like closure, order, and a schedule. They make decisions quickly and get things out of the	Perceiving folks like freedom and a flexible schedule. If plans change, they adapt. They are slower to make

way. Their lives are more ordered.	decisions and don't feel as much need for closure.

For a free version go to: www.personalityjunkie.com This is a good website for more information on your type.

Also offering a free version: www.similarminds.com (listed as Jung tests)

To take the official Myers-Briggs Indicator for around $50, go to: www.mbticomplete.com/en/index.aspx

Knowing Your Type Is An Important Step in Knowing Yourself

Benefits of learning your type:

- You know yourself better and accept yourself better.

- You see your strengths and gifts more clearly.

- You have a way of understanding others. (This boosts your maturity level when you accept and even appreciate how others are different.)

- You can zero in on what careers and jobs are a better match for you.

- You can stop envying others and enjoy developing and using your gifts.

Do a computer search. Enter: Myers-Briggs ESFJ (or whatever your type is) to find a description of your particular type.

Four Stories which Illustrate the Preferences

An Extravert – Introvert Story

A family had moved to a new city and the introverted mother was quite worried about her son who was to begin high school. She wondered how long it would take him to meet friends. A few days later she heard from someone else that on her son's first day at the new school, he stood up on the cafeteria table at lunch and said, "Hi, I'm Leo Barry, how do you like me so far?" Mom didn't realize making friends for her young extravert would not be a problem. (Kroeger, 1988, p. 160)

A Sensing - Intuitive Story

One day I got off work early and decided to buy some more St. Augustine grass to replace grass killed by a heavy winter. When I arrived at the nursery, the only St. Augustine they had was yellow and marked down real cheap. It was the right price, and the man who helped me said it should come back well if I put plenty of water on it. Being intuitive, I could almost see it starting to green up as we loaded it into my Buick's trunk. As I prepared the soil and planted, I started to doubt, since it was so dry and yellow: "Maybe I shouldn't have bought it. No, I'm sure it will be fine."

About that time, my six-year-old son came walking out the front door and down the sidewalk to where I worked. A sensing boy of few words, he stated:

"Ya got some bad grass, Dad."

With that he turned and walked back in the house. My shoulders dropped as I thought,

"I knew I shouldn't have bought that grass."

Sensing people, even at age six, see reality, and call it like it is. Intuitive people love to dream about the possibilities.

A Thinking vs. Feeling Story

I once served on our church elder board. When we had to make personnel or program decisions which would be controversial and hard for some members to accept, the thinker elders would almost always vote objectively and logically. If a program or a person was not working out, they would vote to discontinue the program or terminate the staff member. It seemed obvious to them that decisive action had to be taken. Those of us elders who were feelers would sensitively focus on the emotional impact on the people involved and usually vote to give the program or the staff member more time to improve.

It became so predictable – because of how thinkers make decisions and how feelers make decisions.

A Judging vs. Perceiving Story

I once did a Myers-Briggs seminar for couples. Some of our couple friends attended. With one of these couples, the husband was a J (judging) and the wife was a P (perceiving). During the seminar, I talked about how to live with a J and how to live with a P.

A couple of weeks later, I saw the husband, and he told me he would chronically get irritated with his wife because, as they went their separate ways for work in the morning, he would always ask her what she wanted to do for dinner that night. Being a J he wanted a plan — if they were going out to eat or staying home. He would become frustrated every morning that she couldn't give him a simple answer. After the seminar he understood that, as a P, she didn't have as much of a need to plan, and she sure didn't like to make quick decisions without some time to think.

The husband happily informed me he now leaves her a note with some options to think about and asks her to call him when she's ready to say what she prefers. It works much better for both. Now he gets it. She's not being stubborn or difficult. She (P) just approaches life in a different way than he does, and that's okay.

Knowing Yourself: A Foundational Stone

This book is about knowing yourself. Toward that goal, learning your Myers-Briggs type is a foundational stone from which you can build on your strengths and gifts. I've observed that most people, by age fifty, have figured out by trial and error, what they are good at and what they're not so good at.

My desire is that you shave a few years off that trial and error learning by understanding your temperament and type.

I can recall that at age twenty-five, I thought I could be good at administrative tasks. I thought I could be good at leadership. Years later, I realized those were not my strengths. My ego aspired to those things, and at times I strived for those things, but it was like putting on clothes that didn't fit. I wasn't comfortable, and I probably looked funny.

The Rabbit, the Turtle, and the Duck

Once there was a rabbit, a turtle, and a duck starting first grade. The very first day they went through assessments. School personnel measured four areas: running, swimming, flying, and jumping.

First they tested the rabbit and found that he was very good at running and jumping, but very weak in swimming and flying. They put him in flying classes.

Next, they tested the turtle and found was good at swimming, but weak in running, jumping, and flying. They put him in running classes.

The final assessment revealed that the duck was skilled in flying, decent at swimming, but poor at running and jumping, so they put him in jumping classes.

The rabbit, turtle, and duck worked very hard all through first grade. Finally, the big day came to test again to find out how much each had improved. The rabbit still could not fly. The turtle still could not run fast. And the duck couldn't jump. Everyone, including the teachers, felt like a failure.

The moral of story: don't waste a year trying to do something you were never designed to do. If the rabbit had worked on his jumping, if the turtle had worked on his swimming, if the duck had worked on his flying, then huge improvements would have been realized, because that is exactly what they were designed to do.

We Grow Up Focusing on What We Can't Do

I realize in our schools we need to teach basic skills and core courses. I applied myself and strove for good grades, but I worried and stressed about my weak areas: algebra II, chemistry, and foreign language – I felt pretty dumb sometimes. And most of the kids placed in special education, felt totally dumb. In reality, they had an undiagnosed learning disability.

In the 1980's and 1990's educators and diagnosticians made huge strides in identifying learning disabilities and reducing the stigma. At some point, it dawned on me: a person could be weak in most academic subjects, yet still be competent and successful in a single occupation. They just had to find the occupation that is a match for their aptitudes and skills.

Albert Einstein once said, "Everybody is a genius. But if you judge a fish by its ability to climb a tree, it will live its whole life believing that it is stupid."

Conclusion

Can you see why I appreciate this tool — the Myers-Briggs Type Indicator? It gives you a jump-start on knowing your temperament and your type. It helps you be more clear on your natural personality tendencies and strengths. It also helps you know some of your weaknesses and areas where you are not gifted.

Questions for Reflection and Discussion

- How do you know yourself better after reading this chapter?

- Are you a duck who has tried to be a rabbit? Explain.

- Name two strengths you are now more aware of having learned about the Myers-Briggs.

- Can you see how you might have been expecting others to be like you? Give one example.

- What preference would you like to develop further and why?

Chapter 5

More Insights from the Myers-Briggs

Four Temperaments within the Sixteen Types

Another gift developing out of the Myers-Briggs is the concept of four temperaments. This was developed by Keirsey and Bates and presented in *Please Understand Me* and *Please Understand Me II*. Below are their four temperaments. One temperament should be a fit for you. (Keirsey & Bates, 1984), (Keirsey D. , 1998)

The SJ Guardians ESTJ ESFJ ISTJ ISFJ

The SJ Guardian folks include S (sensing) and J (judging) among their four Myers-Briggs temperment. Traditional, orderly, work before play, these are the solid citizens, the responsible ones who find meaning in serving and being useful. Security is important, and they tend to have a lot of "parent" in them, possessing strong values about how life should be. SJs seek more traditional settings such as established institutions with clear structure and procedures. Education, banking, government work, accounting, hospitals, administrators, and managers are some natural choices that fit the SJ Guardian. Think Guardian of tradition and order.

The SP Artisans
ESTP ESFP ISTP ISFP

The SP Artisans are practical and usually good with their hands. Their philosophy is "Eat, drink and be merry, for tomorrow we may die." They are spenders, not savers like the SJs. They live in the present and resist being bound by demands or a constraining schedule. They are the spontaneous free spirits. They have a lot of child in them. SPs gravitate toward hands-on careers like the trades, music, art, cooking, or sports, to name a few. Think working with your hands on something real, earthy, or fun – the Artisan.

The NF Idealists
ENFJ ENFP INFJ INFP

The NF Idealists are the sensitive dreamers who get excited about the possibilities. They want meaning in what they do. They want to make a difference in the world. They value their own growth and development. They support and encourage the growth of others. NFs often enjoy the helping professions, teaching, acting or the ministry. They like to use their creative energies and compassion to help people grow and develop. Think warm, encouraging, creative – the Idealists.

The NT Rationals
ENTJ ENTP INTJ INTP

The NT Rationals are intellectual and are attracted to complex problems. They make decisions based on what is true and what is logical. They can be less than sensitive to the feelings of others. Just as they value their own intellectual growth and acquisition of knowledge, they urge the same for those they care about. Often creative with ideas and technology, NTs gravitate toward careers requiring complex knowledge, and continual research and learning. This could include science, law, medicine, research, engineering, a college professor, or a technically oriented business, to name a few. Think knowledge, intellect – the Rationals.

Practical Application: How the Myers-Briggs Helped Our Marriage

I mentioned above that I am an INFP and my wife, Lalla, is an ESFJ. As an INFP, I am the Idealist temperament. As an ESFJ, she is a Guardian. Understanding our types gave us important insights, that helped us know each other in a deeper way. It helped us understand our marriage. Here's the story:

> After our first child was born, we bought a larger home that we could "grow into." While stretched to make the payments, we loved the house and the property with trees and a creek. Since money was tight, it would take us a few years to completely furnish the bigger home.
>
> As an intuitive (N), thinking about the future and how it would look someday, was enough for me to be content with the present. Being perceiving (P), with little need for closure, the unfinished state of the house didn't bother me. Also as an introverted intuitive (IN), I tended to be the absent-minded professor who was in my head, thinking about more abstract ideas, rather oblivious to my immediate environment. As an INFP psychologist, I was more focused on buying books of clinical interest and going to training conferences to pick up new skills, so I could better help my clients.
>
> Since money was tight, Lalla would have to sign-off on these books and trainings. She would usually support my book and conference expenditures because as an ESFJ, she was service-oriented and had a strong desire to support me and encourage me in my career and training.
>
> But every few months, Lalla would have a little frustration crisis with some tears, because we didn't have enough money to furnish and decorate the house. Before learning about the Myers-Briggs, I was a little surprised by this because she was usually a happy, upbeat person who was a great mom, and so supportive of me. After we took the Myers-Briggs, I started to understand what it was like for her.
>
> Here she is, a stay-at-home mom, at least while the kids are pre-school aged. She is an extraverted sensing (ES) person who has a heightened awareness of her environment. She is judging (J), so she likes closure and getting things finished. She is at home much

of the day, and as an ESFJ, is much more visually aware of things around her and how the decorating and furnishings look. But I am only there in the evening and not that aware (IN) of my environment. Also, I have little need for closure (P), so it doesn't bother me.

No wonder Lalla would get so frustrated! She also had an internal conflict because as an ESFJ wife, she wanted to serve me and support my desire for books and conferences, yet the more she did that, the more it delayed decorating the home. The Myers-Briggs gave us a tremendous insight into what was going on and helped me balance money for conferences with money for decorating.

The Personality Gap
Marriage, Colleagues, Friends

Bob (ESTP) and Sally (ESFJ) score the following intensities on the Myers-Briggs. You can see they are both extraverts, and they are both sensing. However, they have different preferences for thinking versus feeling and different preferences for judging versus perceiving. I call the difference between them, their personality gap.

	MIDPOINT			
EXTRAVERT	Bob Sally			INTROVERT
SENSING	Sally	Bob		INTUITION
FEELING	Sally		Bob	THINKING
JUDGING		Sally	Bob	PERCEIVING

Where do they have the largest personality gap? Sally is a strong feeler and Bob is a strong thinker. There is a big gap between their scores. They make decisions in a very opposite way. This may be a big area of frustration and conflict for them if they don't understand where the other is coming from.

The other obvious gap is Sally is a J and Bob is a P. They are going to have some "odd couple" struggles around schedule, order, and neatness.

But since they are both extraverts and both sensing, there is not much gap in these areas. Thus, they may operate smoothly, because they are alike and understand each other.

While I have illustrated the personality gap with a couple, it is relevant for any relationship. It would be great if parents had insight into their particular personality gaps with their youngsters. They would likely still see the same behavior, but be less judging and more understanding.

For example, an ISTJ ten-year-old boy might keep his room ship-shape most of the time. However, an ENFP ten-year-old girl might have too many creative projects and relationships to enjoy, and not even notice the messy condition of her room. ENFP children will need more structure and supervision to keep their rooms in decent order. But if a parent can supervise from their calm Adult ego state rather than their harsh Critical Parent, the room will be in better order, and so will their relationship.

Back to the Myers-Briggs and Living Your Design

My point is, none of us has the gifts of all sixteen types. But we do have the gifts of our one type, our unique design. This is part of the exhilaration of discovering yourself and developing yourself. This is part of discovering and living more out of the "True Self," that will be presented next, in chapter six. To the extent we don't know our true type and try to mimic or dress up in other types, we are beating our heads against a wall and missing our lives.

Correlation from Scripture: Spiritual Gifts

Four passages in the New Testament explain spiritual gifts (Romans 12, 1 Corinthians 12, Ephesions 4, and 1 Peter 4). I don't think there is a specific, limited number of spiritual gifts. I say this because the listings of gifts in the four passages noted above include different gifts in different passages. I think the writers are teaching that each believer has gifts and that we are not all gifted the same, but that the Body of Christ needs the various gifts to be functioning.

The Apostle Peter put it this way:

> God has given each of you a gift from his great variety of spiritual gifts. Use them well to serve one another. [11] Do you have the gift of speaking? Then speak as though God himself were speaking through you. Do you have the gift of helping others? Do it with all the strength and energy that God supplies. Then everything

you do will bring glory to God through Jesus Christ. (1 Peter 4:10-11, The New Living Bible)

We see the concept of people being gifted differently and needing one another's gifts/personalities as a principle from Scripture as well as from secular sources like the Myers-Briggs.

Integrating T.A.'s Five Ego States with Myers-Briggs

Truth tends to integrate. Let me share some correlations I often see between T.A.'s five ego states and the Myers-Briggs.

CRITICAL PARENT	Those who are SJs tend to have a lot of critical parent styles. They have a strong sense of "should." It's just part of their temperament. They have to be careful to not be controlling with others.
NURTURING PARENT	Those with NF or SF preferences tend to be pretty warm and encouraging. Throw in a little E (extraversion), and you've got the ultimate nurturing.
ADULT	Thinkers (T). Logical. Analytical. Cool. Objective.
FREE CHILD	Those fun-loving SP's. They know how to have a good time right now.
ADAPTED CHILD	Feelers (F) can be such pleasers, and so can extraverts(E) because they want everyone to like them.
REBELLIOUS CHILD	SPs can be a little rebellious to authority. "Don't impinge on my freedom." Mix in some introverted thinkers (IT), who have little need to please. If a thinking, judging type(TJ) already has a plan, they can come across as rebellious and stubborn.

Am I Focusing too Much on Self Discovery?

In case any Christian readers fear I've gone a little too humanistic and am off track on a self-discovery, "Aren't I wonderful?" trip, allow me to address that concern.

I am discouraging you from pursuing something that is not really you (False Self). I am encouraging you to pursue and develop your original God-given design. I believe your Myers-Briggs type gives you specific information regarding your design. Your gifts come from God. Enjoy them and use them, and they will expand and grow.

Don't focus on what you can't do. Don't envy the gifts you don't have. Enjoy and pursue your design. You will be surprised and delighted when assessed at the end of the year (in contrast to the rabbit, the turtle, and the duck).

When I talk about finding your True Self, I'm talking about a normal developmental process we all need to go through. According to Jung, much of the first half of life we are developing the ego. In light of more recent psychology I see the ego as related to the False Self.

The concepts of True Self and False Self will be explained more fully in the next chapters. Still, I believe all Christians come to their end – to the end of their ego-lives. We realize life is more than ego accomplishments. We get the great job or we get the big house, and we are still empty and insecure. Hopefully, we come not just to believe in God, but we come to a point of intimacy with God and letting Him into every part of our lives. Christ in us grows, and ego fades.

The Body Is Dying, The Ego Is Dying

Just because our bodies are aging and eventually breaking down, we don't neglect and abuse them. We take care of our bodies and know for the Christian, the body is the temple (housing) of the soul and spirit. Similarly, when we are young our ego develops and becomes proficient; it helps with many important life functions. Yet, to mature and follow God, our ego-led life must fade, and even in a sense, die, just like our bodies will someday die. As long as we are living, we will have our ego, but for the Christian it is more like Vice President of Operations. We don't get rid of our ego any more than we get rid of our brain or our heart, but our ego becomes more under the yoke of Christ. John the Baptist, referring to Jesus, said, "He must increase, but I must decrease." (ESV, John 3:30)

Questions for Reflection and Discussion

- Which of the Myers-Briggs temperaments (SJ, SP, NF, NT) do you feel is yours? Explain how this has helped you know yourself better?

- Think of a friend or family member who is a different temperament. How will this help understand them and get along better?

- Can you think of someone with whom you have a "personality gap," someone with whom you clash or where you seem to frustrate and misunderstand one another? How do you think understanding your personality differences on the various preferences helps you understand and appreciate each other better?

Chapter 6

A "Self" Is Developed

Have you ever wondered why some people are secure and have a direction to their lives? They seem to know who they are and be comfortable in their own skins, while others are insecure and drifting, never solid, stable, or confident.

My goal is to give you a psychologically sound answer to that question. Get ready for a crash course in "how to raise a healthy child". But first, a little story.

The Baby Whisperer

Recently my sister and her husband spent a few hours with our thirty-three-year-old daughter and her young family. Our daughter, Sarah, and her husband, J.R., have three kids under seven years of age. The youngest is six months old.

Near the end of their visit, my brother-in-law asked J.R., "Little Campbell is so calm and happy. And the two older ones play so well together. How do ya'll do it?"

"It helps to have 'the baby whisperer' for my wife," said J.R., referring to Sarah.

Of course we smiled when we heard a nice compliment on our daughter. Lalla, and I had the opportunity to study the basics of child development before we had children. Sarah, our oldest, was born during my psychology internship.

Throughout Sarah's early life and childhood, we tried to apply what I had learned in graduate school about child development and childrearing. Every parent makes mistakes, and we tried to correct some of the parenting mistakes we felt our parents made. One example, we wanted our kids to know their feelings and express them in good, appropriate ways.

At the dinner table one night when Sarah was about four, something happened, and she said, "That makes me angry."

My mouth almost dropped open. I was amazed she was simply stating the anger she was feeling, and very appropriately. I envied her. She was ahead of me. At age thirty-four, I still struggled to recognize, much less express, my anger. I was stunned, but very pleased that she could do that. It seemed to be no big thing to her. Lalla was a stay at home Mom those years. I knew she must be doing a good job.

A few years later, as a young teenager, Sarah was in a rush to grow up. When we would say "No" or hold her back, she would be angry and express it, sometimes not so appropriately. We had to review what was appropriate. But there was no question, we were dealing with someone who had their own thoughts and needs and opinions. There was no doubt there was a "strong Self" emerging.

Roller Coaster Ride

I'm not saying it was always easy, raising a child who has been given permission to know and share her feelings. Reflecting on it, I get this mental picture of Lalla and me in a roller coaster car, hanging on for dear life as we see Sarah racing ahead of us in her own car. She is screaming with excitement. We are screaming with fear.

We got through those years by praying a lot and asking God for wisdom and protection. By seventeen, she had gone through the rebellious years and was becoming more responsible and respectful. We also made it through this because we knew from our studies of child development that she was merely completing a normal developmental task for a teen. She needed to separate and differentiate from her parents.

Even through her rebellious years, Sarah loved to babysit. And the kids and parents loved her. In college she majored in child development. Her college job was at a day care center, working with three year olds. In her senior year, she decided to be an elementary school teacher. She loved it, and again, the kids loved her. After four years with first and second graders, she had her first baby and became a stay-at-home mom. So that's how she has developed to be the "baby whisperer."

Let me be clear. It's not about being the perfect parent and certainly not about raising perfect children. The perfect child is neither emotionally healthy nor normal. Being a good parent is more about:

- Working on your own growth and becoming emotionally healthy yourself

- Understanding what your child needs and what is going on behind their behavior

- Providing a home that has structure and rules, but also encourages awareness and expression of children's feelings and needs

You are teaching and showing them how to take care of themselves and how to have constructive relationships.

Have I Made My Case?

Knowing about healthy child development is relevant to how well you know yourself. Studying may raise your awareness of the good things you got from your parents and also awareness of what you missed. Of course, it is crucial information if you are a parent.

So sip some more coffee and soak this in slowly. Here is a short course in how the child develops a healthy self.

Ideal Parenting Scenario

Enjoy the Baby

- The couple wants a baby.

- They delight in the new baby.

- They give the messages:

    "I enjoy you as you are."

    "I love you, even when you mess up."

Set Your Needs Aside For Now

- Ideal parents have the maturity to set aside their needs to meet the child's needs.

- Time and attention are given.

- Parental stress and frustration get processed elsewhere, not directed toward the child.

Encourage Expression, Provide Structure

- Ideal parents provide structure and routines to help the little one feel secure.

- The child is encouraged, as they become verbal, to ask for what they need and say what they feel.

- Parents teach age-appropriate skills.

- Parents teach toddlers they sometimes have to wait to get their needs met because mommy and daddy have things they have to do.

- Young children are given a safe environment to play and explore.

- Lots of different play and learning opportunities are provided.

- Parents watch with delight and support as the child's interests and abilities emerge.

Teaching and Setting Limits

- The ideal parent gives the child little chores to do as part of the family.

- Responsibilities and privileges are added as the child ages.

- The ideal parent continues to set limits and protect the adolescent who feels "bulletproof" while reaching for independence and adulthood.

- When the child/teen is rebellious and challenging, the ideal parent stays steady and calm, not reacting emotionally or in a controlling way.

- Ideal parents have principles and a value system that they live by and teach in "sound-bites" at appropriate times. No long lectures please!

Launching and Encouraging

- Parents continue to support the young person's interests and passions by serving as a resource to help them develop.

- The ideal parent doesn't take over these developmental steps toward adulthood, but is a resource and gives the message, "I believe you can do it."

- Ideal parents help their child feel recognized, accepted, and encouraged. The young person leaves the nest with a strong sense of self, because their unique temperament, personality, abilities, and interests have been valued. They don't feel neglected or controlled, but valued and supported so their emerging "self" has been fed and nurtured and is growing and robust.

- The ideal parent is delighted, but also grieving as they let go.

The Healthy, "Differentiated Self"

This kind of parenting gives youngsters the best chance of having a strong, secure sense of "self." The result is children who are fully functional, able to process their feelings, think through problems, develop healthy relationships, take care of themselves, and develop career paths that fit their personalities and gifting. And they are set-up to continue their healthy development.

Dr. Murray Bowen, famed family therapist, used the phrase, "the differentiated self," in describing the young adult coming from a healthy family. Differentiated means the person has separated or differentiated from the family of origin and from others. Bowen described this type of person as secure, content, and non-defensive in their own unique identity. They are able to move easily between being close to people and being separate from people. (Bowen, 1985, p. 529)

"I Want My Regular Bat"

Years ago, I was an assistant coach for my son's fourth-grade baseball team. We made it to the city championship game. Our boys were a little awestruck and intimidated, since we were playing the best team. In the first inning, most of our boys stood there with the bat on their shoulders, hesitant to swing. Standing strikeouts. Not good.

Coach Mike, a 6'5" former college football player, chewed the boys out pretty good. He gave the following order for their next bat, "I want each of you boys to pick a bat smaller than you usually use, and I want to see you up there swinging."

His face was red, and anytime a coach's face is red, well, you know he means business.

His message must have hit home, because in the second inning our boys were swinging and hitting. Our next batter up was ten-year-old Wesley. He was stocky, athletic, and popular with the other boys despite being rather low key. Wesley stepped to the plate with the bases loaded. With a count of two balls and two strikes, Wesley suddenly stepped out of the batter's box, looked back at the ump, and called "Time Out." He turned and slowly walked toward the dugout. I coached first base and wondered, "What the heck is Wesley doing?"

Walking to Coach Mike, Wesley looked up and said, "I want my regular bat."

Coach Mike growled, "Well, go ahead. Get it."

After he retrieved his bat, Wesley walked back to the plate and belted a triple into right center field. Three runners crossed home plate.

The boys went on to win that game 8-3, taking the city championship.

Wesley demonstrated a "healthy self" in action. He knew his swing just didn't feel right with that lighter bat, so he called time out and stopped the game. He then asked his intimidating coach for what he needed – his regular bat. I thought it was pretty amazing that a ten-year-old could do that.

Some Call It the True Self

Other writers have called this "healthy, differentiated self," the True Self. The child who has grown up in the ideal scenario described earlier in the chapter will be able to experience their True Self. Of course this ideal scenario is just that – an ideal. Parents don't always know and do the right thing. But there are degrees along the continuum from the ideal to the unhealthy.

Suggested Reading

Parenting with Love and Logic (Series) by Foster Cline and Jim Fay

The Five Love Languages of Children by Gary Chapman

Questions for Reflection and Discussion

- Reflecting on the ideal parenting scenario, can you name some things your parents did that helped you grow into an independent self?

- Can you think of something you might have missed in childhood that limited the development of the healthy self?

- In adolescence, did you lean toward the Adapted Child (from the chapter on five ego states) or the Rebellious Child, always questioning and pushing the limits?

- How did your parents handle your behavior? Did they seem to understand the normal development you were going through?

- How well were you able to discover who you were (True Self)? What you liked and didn't like? What opinions and beliefs you had which might have been different from your parents? Were you fortunate enough to feel loved and supported through those teen years?

Chapter 7

A Lack of "Self" – the False Self

The first psychiatrist to write about False Self was Donald Winnicott, who saw the creation of the False Self as being an adaptation to the mother's needs and projections. Charles Whitfield and others have offered further explanation: Parents who are emotionally wounded or immature will at times take their frustration out on the child, or they will use the child for their needs. (Whitfield, 1987)

The young, dependent child needs to think of his parents as good, so he takes their critical, shaming messages and sees himself as bad or not good enough. So the False Self is developed with the belief that "If I can be good enough or perfect enough, I will be loved and taken care of."

We Learn to Package Ourselves

David Benner, a psychologist writing from the Christian perspective, describes the creation of the False Self. He says as children we learn we can manipulate the truth about ourselves. We can be afraid but act brave. We can be bad but appear good. We learn to package ourselves. Benner explains that the pretending, which began as an act or a role, gradually becomes part of our identity. We have confused the mask with our real feelings or behavior. (Benner D. G., 2004, p. 78)

Alexander Lowen wrote about the narcissistic personality who lives almost totally out of the False Self. The narcissist's False Self is all about image and success and being one up on people. Remember one camera manufacturer's marketing slogan, "Image is everything."

Inside, the narcissist is empty, not knowing what he feels and not really knowing what love is. The True Self is weak and malnourished, shut away. True intimacy, which is based on mutual sharing of a range of feelings, some happy and some sad or scary, is not something he can do. The narcissist's way of doing a relationship is finding someone who can admire him and stroke his ego. (Lowen, 2012)

Keith Miller, in *The Secret Life of the Soul*, masterfully explained how the False Self, which he calls the "constructed self," is unconsciously created to gain love or esteem. Miller explains, "The child begins secretly to construct another personality, one that is false but appears to be more adequate, intelligent, and/or honest than the child actually is". (Miller, 1997, p. 64)

He shares the story of a lady he calls Janice who felt she was not getting the same love and attention that her father gave two older brothers. She basically became a tomboy, mastering the sports activities of her brothers, to obtain her father's attention. Later, she discovered that "...underneath it all, I am very feminine and like being a woman."

Since reading Lowen many years ago, I thought of the False Self as only related to the narcissist. Keith Miller explains how the False Self can take many different forms. For example, the False Self in another may be someone who falls into the role of "victim," taking the blame and keeping the peace to avoid confrontations. The child adopts the behavior to calm the angry, abusive parent. The family seems to get along better if one child is the scapegoat. (Miller, 1997, p. 68)

Unfortunately, this often gets carried throughout life, when it is no longer needed. It can be hard and scary to dismantle the False Self when the True Self is so weak and undeveloped.

Now, let's do a more in-depth examination of the unhealthy parent scenario. Or we could call this "how miss-guided parenting helps create a False Self."

Unhealthy Parenting Scenario

Baby Is a Lot of Trouble

- The unhealthy parents don't want the baby or wanted the baby for the wrong reasons.

- The parent views the baby as an interruption or bother.

- Or, the parent has many expectations and may view baby as a possession.

I Can Make Him Mind Me

- The unhealthy parent sees the baby as something to be trained or controlled.

- The parent is critical and negative in setting limits and correcting.

- The parent may be openly disappointed in the child Parent when expectations are not met.

- The parent uses "shaming voices," which the child internalizes, setting up poor self-esteem, hiding, and striving.

- The parent sees the child as mostly a big stress or responsibility, not a delight and joy.

I'm Glad When He Entertains Himself

- The unhealthy parent fails to give the child proper attention, time, nurturing, and play.

- The child of unhealthy parents may lack limits and be over-indulged because it is easier on the parent to just "give them what they want," or because the parent doesn't want the child to be angry. The child may feel like he is the king and running things. This actually fills the child with anxiety because he knows he is inadequate to be running things. Inside the child may be thinking, "Somebody stop me. Doesn't anybody care?"

- Without parental support, the child has to figure out how to get love and attention. His unconscious solution may be positive or negative attention.

My Child Makes Me Look Good

- Unhealthy parents may use the child and the child's abilities or talents to enhance their own image. They may train their kids to perform. The child learns he gets the love and attention he/she wants – if she is really pretty, or really good in sports, school, or music. The unhealthy parent attends to and reinforces behavior that enhances the parent's image

- Children of unhealthy parents learn that certain needs or feelings or interests are very negative so they begin suppressing their feelings. This is the birth of the False Self. It is not usually a conscious thought or conscious decision. They simply decide they will put more energy and focus into the activities and behaviors that get their parents' attention and approval. The little True Self goes into hiding and gets little attention or encouragement. It is the runt of the personality and may seldom be seen. It hangs back in the shadows as life moves forward, with the False Self taking center stage

- This development of the False Self may be followed by lying and/or hiding behavior that doesn't get rewarded or that would bring criticism and disappointment

Remember...the False Self Can Have Many Versions

Here are some frequent False Self identities:

- Narcissist – I'm superior to you, Let me count the ways.

- Victim – I'm helpless, mistreated, and used.

- Peacemaker – I calm people down. I manage angry feelings.

- Giver – I'm committed to helping others, whatever they want or need.

- Hero – I'm strong, and I'll swoop in and save the day.

- Intellectual – I'm smart, and I can think. Knowledge is my forté.

- Beauty – I'm special because of my beautiful face/body.

- Athlete – I'm gifted in sports. That's where I excel.

- Spiritual One - I am good and pure and only seek Godly things.

- Lazy One - I'm laid back, taking it easy, "Let George do it."

- Workaholic – I can get it done, no matter how long it takes.

- Party Guy – I know how to have a good time. That's what it's all about.

- _____

- _____

- _____

Questions for Reflection and Discussion

- Can you recognize some tendency in yourself to try to impress others and look a certain way while hiding other aspects of yourself you don't want them to see? Think about or discuss the image or False Self you were trying to be.

- Can you connect this image (False Self) with what your parents or your culture seem to value and promote? Explain.

- As you grew older, in your twenties or thirties, did you become aware that there were things you liked or enjoyed that you weren't free to feel or be when you were younger?

Chapter 8

The False Self: Stories of Collapse

While the False Self helps us cope, it is performance based. It has been our god, our way of trying to control life and find security and love. When we experience major life stresses, our False Self, our ego strategies, may begin to unravel. We feel our lives falling apart. This crisis can lead to transformation as we move from an ego run life, to a healthier, more secure way of living. But first, we must open our eyes to our ingrained ways of coping. It is a scary process – like letting go of a familiar trapeze bar, and reaching for the new bar. Can we trust living from of our True Self? Can we trust God for security in life instead of trusting our False Self?

Story One: Sue Monk Kidd

Sue Monk Kidd is a popular writer, novelist, and memoirist. Perhaps most widely known for her novel, *The Secret Life of Bees* that prompted a movie. Kidd's first book was a memoir, *God's Joyful Surprise* about discovering God's grace. Her second book, *When the Heart Waits*, was a treasure, rich with insights for our study of knowing yourself. Here, Sue vulnerably shares her struggle to know herself and to know God in a new way. Despairing and stuck in her Christian growth, she questioned her identity, her ego-made life.

In Kidd's words,

- I dragged myself to a little bench wedged among the trees. Sitting there, I studied their bony arms and felt their emptiness, their desperate reach for sky and light. Tears rimmed my eyes and burned on my cheeks. It made no sense.

I'd never really believed in midlife crises. But here I was having one, and it was frighteningly real.

- The familiar circles of my life left me with a suffocating feeling. My marriage suddenly seemed stale, unfulfilling; my religious structures, stifling. My life had curled up in to the frightening mark of a question. (Kidd S. M., 2006, p. 5)

Through her readings, she realized God brought her into a period of waiting. A scary question formed:

Is it possible that I am being summoned from some deep and holy place within? Am I being asked to enter a new passage in the spiritual life – the journey from False Self to True Self? Am I being asked to dismantle old masks and patterns and unfold a deeper, more authentic self – the one God created me to be? (Kidd S. M., 2006, p. 8)

Here we are reminded of Jung's view from Chapter Two on the Ego. He saw the "morning of life" as our ego learning to maneuver the tasks of the outer world such as making a living and finding social support. The "afternoon of life" deals with the inner world by developing the True Self. He likened this process, often coming out of some mid-life crisis, to a difficult birth. A new self emerges. The "old ego self" recedes from prominence.

Sue Monk Kidd notes, "We need reassurance that it's okay to let the old masks die, to 'pluck up' what was planted long ago." She was encouraged in her digging and plucking by the writings of Thomas Merton:

One's actual self may be far from "real," since it may be profoundly alienated from one's own deep spiritual identity. To reach one's "real self" one must, in fact, be delivered from that illusory and false 'self' whom we have created. (Kidd S. , 2006, p. 30)

Merton and others believe the more our True Self emerges, the more Christ is formed in us. This becomes the path to being more Christ like. As St. Paul wrote: "It is no longer I who live, but Christ who lives in me." (Galatians 2:20)

As Kidd searched to find and question her False Self, she found more than one. She skillfully illustrated her false selves with nursery rhymes, fictional characters, and models from her childhood. Here are two of those false selves:

The first False Self Kidd shares came from a painting of a little dark-haired girl in a blue dress with a sweet smile, and from the poem, *Little Girl with a Curl.*

Good Southern Girl

Sue realized the picture which hung in her room, the poem, and her Southern culture's messages for women, all came together to build this False Self. Girls were to be pleasing, sweet, and demure, getting what they wanted by charm. Good girls were to suppress their own feelings and thoughts, and be what the other person wants them to be. (Kidd, S.M., 2006, pp. 59-60)

Little Red Hen (children's story)

Sue recalled the story of The Little Red Hen, one of her favorites. The Little Red Hen not only did all the inside chores, but she did the outside chores too. One day she found some grains of wheat and asked who would help her plant them. Everyone said, "Not I." So she did it all. Sue explains this is the story of the martyr. No one will help so she does it all. She ends up the bitter, worn-out victim.

Playing this role for many years, she worked so hard to take care of everybody but herself. The weariness and resentment grew, but she felt she had no choice. Change can begin when one slows down enough to become aware of one's feelings and face the martyr role. Sue says that those in *The Little Red Hen*, the False Self needs to address two things: to love oneself, and to learn to play.

Sue recalled a time when she and a friend came upon a deserted playground while walking. They shyly went to the swings and just sat at first with feet dangling. Before long they were swinging high and laughing and singing. "It reunited us with that part of ourselves that's eternally at play with God and life." (Kidd S. M., 2006, pp. 64-67)

Story Two: Brennan Manning

Brennan Manning, born in New York City during the Great Depression, became a Franciscan monk in his twenties. He ministered in several cities in the South before he turned to writing. Author of some twenty books, *The Ragamuffin Gospel,* has been called a classic meditation on grace. An earlier book, *Abba's Child,* is of particular interest to our study as he tells his story of dealing with the False Self. The following excerpts are from Abba's Child.

On the last morning of his twenty day retreat in the Rockies, Manning wrote this letter:

> Good morning, imposter [his False Self].

> I come to you today not with rod in hand but with an olive branch. When I was a little shaver and first knew that no one was there for me, you intervened and showed where to hide.....without your intervention I would have been overwhelmed by dread and paralyzed with fear. You were there for me and played a crucial, protective role in my development. Thank you. (Manning B. , 2002, p. 46)

Manning credits the imposter with helping him build a cottage that became a safe place to play under the covers. There the four year old Brennan felt completely safe and happy while his real world appeared threatening. Manning's letter to imposter continues:

> But in the construction process you taught me how to hide my real self from everyone and continued a lifelong process of concealment, containment, and withdrawal. Your resourcefulness enabled me to survive.

> As the years rolled by, you-I got strokes from a variety of sources. I had neither the perception nor the courage to tame you, so you continued to rumble like Sherman through Atlanta, gathering momentum along the way. Your appetite for attention and affirmation became insatiable. I never confronted you with the lie because I was deceived myself. (Manning B. , 2002, p. 47)

Manning then tells imposter that he will give him a gift – he will take the imposter into the presence of Jesus. Manning notes that in the company of Jesus, the imposter starts looking smaller and smaller, so he nicknames him Pee-Wee. He acknowledges that the imposter served a purpose and got him through some rough times. Manning's growing union with his Father, or Abba-Daddy, as he comes to intimately call him, means the imposter becomes smaller and takes a back seat in Manning's life. (Manning B. , 2002, pp. 47-48)

Story Three: Keith Miller

The late Keith Miller began his writing career with the bestselling, *Taste of New Wine*. Known for his honesty and transparency, he wrote *A Hunger for Healing: The Twelve Steps as a Classic Model for Christian Spiritual Growth*. Some of the inspiration for my book comes from Miller's, *The Secret Life of the Soul*, 1997. Even though I only had the privilege of meeting and visiting with Keith once, he was my mentor over the years through his many books.

Breakdown of the False Self

At age fifty-seven, Keith Miller, popular author and conference speaker, was falling apart. After a terrifying dream at 3:45 am, he stumbled to the nurses' station and into the arms of an older nurse. She just held him and he sobbed. Keith couldn't hold his life together any longer. It was a good thing.

Miller's early morning breakdown in rehab came within hours after family and friends had confronted him on his selfish, controlling, driven behavior. He was initially defensive. After all, his high-performing False Self had brought him recognition and respect. Yet, he came to see that in his intimate relationships, he used people. Living out of his False Self fed his insecurity as he worked to keep a certain image that lacked reality and integrity. In his fear and pain, he knew what they said was true and that his way of operating, his False Self, created a man who hurt those closest to him. It created a man he didn't respect. (Miller, 1997, p. 164)

A Key Experience from Childhood

Keith Miller recalled a painful experience around the dinner table when he was a child of about eight. His dad asked him what he wanted to be when he grew up. Keith excitedly blurted out that he wanted to be a writer. His older brother, an athlete who received a lot of attention from his father, jumped up and ridiculed Keith for such a sissy occupation. His dad smiled. Keith recalled that he never mentioned writing again to his father, and he buried his dream of writing. When Keith started college, he majored in finance in hopes of gaining his father's approval. Upon graduation, he worked in the oil business, like his father, for several years before he found his true (self) calling – writing and speaking to help people know God in an honest and fresh way. (Miller, 1997, p. 77)

Some twelve years after his breaking point in the rehab hospital, Miller wrote *The Secret Life of the Soul*. Toward the end of this book, Keith shared a time he spent four days with fifteen family members at a South Texas dude ranch. One of his adult daughters walked up to him and asked,

> "What's happened to you, Dad?"

> "What do you mean, honey?"

> "Well, you've looked like you were – at peace, this whole time we've been here."

Miller thought about how tense he usually felt around his family, feeling a need to maintain a "tall constructed white knight personality." He smiled and replied softly,

> "That's because I have been at peace."

Miller then thought to himself,

> I could almost hear my soul laughing, because I hadn't noticed I was peaceful, but I had been. I was just being happy and listening in awe to my amazing wonderful family. (Miller, 1997, p. 210)

Story Four: John Shackelford

As I shared in Chapter One, I always had a desire to be good and to be great.

Going to church and not cussing put me in the good camp. I proved my goodness in the fifth grade. A couple of boys in my class told our teacher that all of the boys in class cussed, except for Glenn and me. Somehow, this information went viral.

In my little hometown viral meant a few people found out, one of whom was my mother. She was so proud of me. I quietly beamed. Yes! I felt morally superior, and my image of being good was set.

This identity of being "good" reached new levels when at age seventeen; I decided God called me to be a missionary. I preached at some local churches and headed off to college as a ministerial student. On the outside, I looked good, but on the inside there were ugly things: thoughts/feelings of lust, envy, and pride. I didn't want people to see that side of me, I wanted to appear to be good —so I did my best to hide those thoughts and feelings.

Now the "great" part. My delusion of greatness centered on sports. I loved basketball and football. I was an overachiever. In sports "overachiever" is lingo for someone who is not the most gifted, but who works their tail off. I made all-district in both sports as a sophomore. I felt very proud of this recognition. Looking back I can see much of my success had to do with my coaches and my teammates. But in my mind I took the credit. Being an athlete became a big part of my identity.

While I never performed as top student in my in high school or college, I did the overachiever thing again. I just kept going. I plugged away and finished my doctor of psychology degree when I was twenty-nine. This became another pillar of my identity, being a psychologist, even a Christian psychologist. Again, I felt proud. And I graduated at a time when the respect for Christian psychologists was on the rise.

To me the pinnacle of my goodness and greatness came when I was age forty. I was asked to serve on the elder board at church. This started off well. I wanted to make an impact. I felt I had a lot to offer. I'd read several books on the church, and of course I was a Christian psychologist. While I'd never served on a church staff or been an elder before, I thought I had the answers. I thought I knew myself. But as Solomon wrote in Proverbs, "Pride goes before a fall."

When It All Went Wrong

Have you ever been through one of those seasons when it seems everything has gone wrong? For me the early 1990's felt like a bad dream where I tried to run from some threat, and I just couldn't get my legs to move. Totally helpless.

- Managed mental healthcare moved into the Dallas market and my income dropped by 70 percent. We sold our larger creek lot home and moved to a much smaller house. This was a big loss for our family since our kids had grown up in that home. Just three years before we had built a large, multi-level deck. It was a beautiful place but we could no longer afford to live there.

- My mother had a stroke and died two weeks later.

- At my church, several elders had conflict with the pastor and resigned. I hung in there, but after much conflict and tension, the pastor asked me to step down from the elder board.

- I didn't handle one of my client cases correctly because of my own emotional wounds. I feared repercussions from the client or the state psychology board. I became clinically depressed and began medication. I also began therapy again to work on my dynamics as a victim of sexual abuse from my childhood.

- My teenage daughter went through a rebellious stage. I questioned myself. Had I failed to be a good father? In my world, if something went wrong, it must be my fault.

- Because of lack of clients, I left private practice and joined a Christian counseling center. After a year I had some conflict with the director and she let me go. While relieved to get out of a hard situation, I also felt great shame and a sense of failure.

Shame and Anger

The Sunday after the counseling center director let me go, I forced myself to attend my church where I had once been an elder. My shame was too raw to have eye contact, much less talk with anyone.

As soon as the service ended, I headed straight for the car. For weeks I tried to keep a low profile, sure people could see I was a loser.

Since finances were so tight, we decided to get by on one car. My office was less than a mile from the house so I walked to work. As I trudged to the office, I felt resentment. I felt sorry for myself. I was angry. This wasn't supposed to be happening to me. Why wasn't God providing more income? Some days I had to catch the city bus to get somewhere. I recalled that prior to my financial collapse, I used to drive by bus stops and feel sorry for those waiting for the bus. Now it was me waiting for the bus. I felt so helpless. At age forty-five, I should be at the height of my career and earning potential, and here I am walking to work or catching the city bus. Not having what felt like a necessity was so damn inconvenient. Did I mention I was angry? I had always secretly looked down on people who couldn't overcome their problems. But here I was, just like them. For the first time in my life, I couldn't make it happen. Good? Great? What a cruel joke.

God Chipped Away

God humbled me - chipping away at my pride and my ego. I didn't like it, but I could see it was necessary. I identified with the biblical character, Joseph, who had been a favored child then lost it all.

The financial stress dragged on for several years. We relied too much on high interest credit cards at times. I often tensed up if I used a credit card in front of people, fearing it would be declined. Fortunately, my wife usually had a steady income. My hard time made it a hard time for her too. She shared recently how alone she felt and how responsible she felt during this time. But she was there for me and the family and I appreciated her support. It took years to rebuild my practice. I eventually found a new niche that was in demand. I have come to be much more thankful and content with whatever we have.

A few years after the worst of it, I went to a men's retreat. The retreat was led by the very pastor with whom I had so much tension on the elder board. Here we were, twelve years later, and we had both lost jobs and been through difficult times. The study for the retreat was Psalms. For the last morning of the retreat, he asked us to us write our own Psalm. We read them to the group. This was mine:

IT'S ALL ABOUT...

Oh Lord, how wondrous and grandiose were my plans.

How strong my longings for status and success.

How clever my dreams to get rich and give it away, while remaining humble among regular people.

And all in the name of the successful Christian life.

Of course I'd give God the credit so He could look good too!

Yes, it was all laid out in my mind – as long as I went to church and kept God's rules.

But something went terribly wrong on my road to the top.

My wife was probably the first to notice – damn it!

While I clung to twin threads of pride and denial.

First, none of my schemes to get rich quick even got off the ground.

My kids were great at first, then my daughter burst out with plans of her own – that didn't include parents or God.

Even my son – who used to think I was great – attached elsewhere and thought I was dumb.

And my patients - who were supposed to be appreciatively dependent, just wouldn't get well – my pearls of human wisdom falling to the floor – and carried out each night with the trash.

As the threads finally snapped, this False Self, this shell of a man, cracked and crumpled to the ground – the only thing standing was a scared little boy looking up to God for help.

Like Joseph without his beautiful coat – no one was impressed.

And inconceivable to me as it was, God loved me just like I was.

My loving Father is teaching me that life is not all about me and that I'm not in control and in that truth is great freedom and rest.

My life is slowing down at fifty-five as I learn that sometimes older eyes see more clearly.

I delight in my young adult children – it's God's love.

I pray with my wife at bedtime – that's real intimacy.

I listen to my patients' struggles – and point them toward God.

I walk in the woods – and the experience the peace of God all around me.

I take pictures of His sunsets – and am reminded that it's all about Him and that He loves me as I am.

Great is the Lord!

Great is His love!

Great is the Lord!

Final Comments on this Chapter

This chapter on collapse of the False Self describes a painful, but necessary experience most of us go through at some point. We spend years learning how to make a life for ourselves in career and relationships, then under the stresses of living our particular version of False Self, we collapse. It often feels like death – death of life as we have known it and lived it. Christians aren't exempt from this trial since we have egos just like non-Christians, egos that need to be demoted to V.P status. Only then are we able to embrace the spiritual walk with Christ as He lives in us and we in Him.

Questions for Reflection and Discussion

- Did you identify with a couple of the stories in this chapter? Which ones sounded like you?

- Can you recognize some of your own False Self? Describe how hard you worked to maintain that image.

- Has there been a time in your life where you had a collapse? Did it turn out to be a good thing? Did you find support and understanding as you went through this?

Chapter 9

Reclaiming Lost Parts of the Self

In the mid 90's I attended a conference for Christian psychologists. Dr. Nancy Thurston, a California psychologist, gave a presentation on the importance of helping clients reclaim lost parts of themselves. She shared her story. At age thirty, she vacationed with her husband in Germany. Visiting a large amusement park, she unexpectedly cried, overcome with grief.

Nancy flashed back to a memory of visiting Disneyland as a young girl with a church group. She came home filled with wonder, excited to tell her mother all about Fantasyland and the characters she'd met. She ran upstairs and found her mom inspecting her untidy room. Her mom scolded her for leaving such a mess. Nancy hung her head, engulfed in shame. She didn't tell her mom about the wonderful day. It was all ruined. Some twenty years later, Nancy wept and shared that painful memory with her husband. The amusement park in Germany was designed by Walt Disney. Since that painful moment with her mom twenty years before, she had never let her imagination flow. She had not let herself dream or create. That day, Nancy, crying and talking with her husband, began to reclaim a precious part of her that had been locked away for two decades.

Identifying Two of My Lost Parts

Nancy's story struck a chord in me. I could hardly wait to get back to my hotel room. I pulled a sheet of paper and drew a large circle on it. Then I drew ten circles within the large circle. I filled in each circle with key parts or roles in my life. Husband, father, church member, therapist, psychological examiner, brother, friend, and sports fan — filled eight circles. But I knew something important was missing.

It took me less than sixty seconds to fill in the two empty circles. Carpentry. Writing. Growing up on a small ranch, my dad taught me basic carpenter skills. One summer before my senior year in high school I worked for a local carpenter. I loved it. It was hot in Texas, but there were days I felt disappointed when five o'clock came. I wanted to keep building.

Throughout the first twenty years of my marriage, I only did carpentry work if we needed something, such as a built-in bookcase or a cabinet for the TV. I loved this work but only did it when necessity called. Money was often tight, and building materials and tools were expensive. Also, I wanted my non-work time to be spent largely with our children. Good reasons to not spend extra money. All this time I never let myself dream about building something just because I enjoyed it. I went months without picking up a hammer or a saw.

Writing had always held intrigue for me. As a first-year graduate student in psychology, I thought about writing an article on grief, reflecting on the sudden death of my dad. I never wrote it. I also fantasized about writing a book called *Finding God's Will*. I made the mistake of sharing this with my mom. Mom's comment was, "Shouldn't someone with more experience write a book like that?" I dropped the idea. I figured maybe she was right.

Over the years, I wrote hundreds of psychological reports. Asked to write an article in 1987 for a professional journal, I threw myself into it and did a good job. I even received some nice feedback from the editor, but I didn't continue to write unless someone invited me. I never set aside time to write or study writing just for me.

What's A Lost Part of Self?

A lost part of self, is a part that has been cut off or set aside for some reason. The lost part can wither. Neglected, it doesn't develop or grow with the rest of you. For Nancy Thurston, the lost part was her imagination. For me, it was the creativity of building with wood and building with words.

Since my increased awareness of reclaiming lost parts, I have encouraged my clients to consider this concept and reclaim lost parts of themselves.

Martha, a thirty-five year old mother of three, ran herself ragged. She worked as an administrative assistant during the day, and took care of the little ones at night. Her husband traveled most weeks but was there to help on the weekends. Despite being dog-tired, she couldn't go to bed until the kitchen was clean and the house was in order. She got to bed at midnight or 1 a.m. Martha felt stressed and guilty when her anger spilled out on the kids. She was all Critical Parent and Adult. She had lost her Free Child ego state (Transactional Analysis).

In a couple's session with Martha and her husband, I heard that he had encouraged her to resign from her office job. With permission and support from her husband, Martha was finally able to quit her day job. With some time for herself during the day now, she began to think about her needs. Not only was it okay to take care of herself, but as a thirty-five year old, it was her responsibility to take care of herself.

Discussing lost parts, she recalled how as a child she loved to dance. Martha hadn't danced in years. She rearranged her priorities and joined a dance class for grownup girls. She replaced her resentment with gratitude and joy.

I invite to you think about something you did or loved as a child or young person. Maybe you were discouraged from doing it or you stopped for some reason. It could be poetry, painting, a sport, a craft, reading science fiction, taking a college course, hiking, decorating, fishing... the possibilities are infinite. Anything you felt passionate about.

Lost Parts as Lost Ego States

The busy mother who joined a dance class illustrated a specific activity/passion that was lost. A broader way to think about this is considering lost ego states. Remember the five ego states from Transactional Analysis: Critical Parent, Nurturing Parent, Adult, Free Child, Adapted/Rebellious Child. With many people, their lost part has to do with the Free Child ego state.

Playful Child

Somewhere along the way some people's playful side was criticized or shamed, and it hid. They must let their Fee Child come out and play.

During graduate school we lived in Southern California, not too far from Disneyland. During one of our visits to the famous amusement park, I realized my wife and I were approaching it very differently. When we arrived at the entrance, her Free Child came out to play. She was excited at all she saw. I was quiet and solemn. Somewhere along the way, between childhood and adulthood, I had judged that I was too old to be silly and "act like a kid." It's a fun assignment to let your Free Child come out and play. Reflecting further, I realized my Free Child came out when my favorite sports team made a big play.

Free Child Feelings and Needs

Have you lost touch with your *feelings*? Feelings, built-in from birth, can get suppressed or repressed and, for all practical purposes, lost. Some children receive the message that it's not okay to be angry, sad, hurt, scared, joyous, excited. In reality, these are normal and frequent feelings, and it is good to be aware of them. Remember, it's hard to manage a feeling if you're not aware of it.

Perhaps you learned certain of your *needs* were not okay so you lost touch with them. God made us with needs. Some basic needs are: food, sleep, recreation, affection, intellectual stimulation, and relationships. It's okay to be aware of them. If we're not aware of them and don't take responsibility to meet them, we don't have the supplies we need to live life.

It's good to reclaim your feelings. It's good to reclaim your needs. Working in these areas, you are connecting with instinctual parts of you. If you suppress or repress them, they often pop out in unexpected and sometimes destructive ways.

Ten Years Later

Sadly, it was ten years after hearing Dr. Thurston and drawing those circles, before I began to seriously reclaim my "lost selves." It took two dramatic experiences in the spring of 2002 to get my attention.

Life Is Short

In April of 2002 I was shocked to learn that my longtime friend, Royce Aston, had died of a massive heart attack. Royce was a social worker from my hometown, and he helped me get my first job after college at Methodist Children's Home in Waco. Those two years I worked there, Royce and I, along with six other men, played full-court basketball during the lunch hour three days a week. My memory of Royce, who was seven years my senior, was him sprinting down the court or firing me a long pass. Now it was hard to believe that thirty-five years had flown by and he was gone.

A few weeks later, I attended a conference in Tiburon, California. Tiburon is a beautiful, flower-filled community just across the bay from San Francisco. I studied Heart Rate Variability (HRV), a new biofeedback program to train people to breathe right, relax, and take care of their hearts.

With Royce's heart attack and death still weighing on me, I worried about my own heart. After all, my dad died of a coronary at age fifty-six. I was fifty-three.

At the conference, we partnered up and practiced treating each other with the sophisticated Heart Rate Variability biofeedback. My breathing was not very deep and my heart rate variability numbers looked like I was pretty stressed. I was paired up with a chiropractor who had already been using HRV biofeedback in his practice. I confided in him about my dad's early death and my own fears.

Talking with this chiropractor over the three days, he intuitively picked up on my Until Script. People with an Until Script are always planning to do something they really want to do, but they don't let themselves do it until some responsibility is completed. Some call this a When Script.

For example,

When the kids are, gone I'll buy a bass boat and start fishing.

I won't take a vacation, until I'm totally out of debt.

When I retire, I'm going to drive to Canada.

I won't go back to college, until I'm financially stable.

My Until Script was: *I'd love to build a cabin on the wooded property where I grew up, but I won't do that until we can afford it.* The chiropractor advised me to stop worrying about my heart, and start doing some things now that I was postponing. He said doing some things I had passion about now would be good for my heart. That was some wisdom that I needed to hear. He gave me permission to live now.

Returning to Texas from the HRV conference, I learned that a nineteen year old client of mine died of a heart attack while I was gone. I was stunned. It was like God wrote across the sky in mile high letters "Life Is Short".

Project 1: Tree House

Flying back to Texas from California, I dreamed about building a cabin on my wooded acreage. For the first time, I thought about actually doing it. But how would I start? What could I do right now? Then it came to me: the first step was to cut a trail through the woods. Arriving home, I bought an $80 pair of heavy-duty pruners. Over the next month I made a couple of trips to the property and cut the trail for a few hours, and soon, my trail was complete.

I can't emphasize enough how big that first step was for me. Making a dream a reality always begins with one do-able step. What was once a "someday fantasy" became now, became real. From a lost passion, to an exciting first step.

Three years later, I read about big treehouses. There were beautiful pictures. I thought, "That's it. I will build a big treehouse so we have a place to stay on our property. It will be so cool." I spent almost a year clearing brush and trees to make a road. The road wound through the trees, across the creek, and up through the forest to the top of our property. The giant live oak tree I chose was in a large grove of live oaks and cedars. According to my plans, I would build up from the heavily wooded hilltop, but the upper level of the treehouse would look out over the treetops.

Today, the treehouse is 98 percent finished. It has two levels and is nearly 500 square feet. The vista is of the northern Texas Hill Country. Most of it was completed working about four hours a week for six years. I loved the designing and the building. I learned so much about building. I did things I'd never done before. I developed my carpentry skills and enjoyed it along the way. My wife, Lalla, my adult kids, and grandkids love it too. I'm the Tree House Guy.(There I go again, turning it into a False Self identity. Really it was a longing deep within which God allowed me to enjoy) It was a lost part, reclaimed and developed.

Project 2: Writing

My writing efforts, in contrast to my treehouse, had never gotten off the ground. Oh, I'd dabbled here and there. I wrote a handful of humorous skits and stories. I even took two online writing courses, but I'd never committed to writing until three years ago.

In June of 2012 I attended my first North Texas Christian Writers' Conference. Though a novice, I boldly entered one of my stories in their contest. I thought my story pretty good, at least my family and friends liked it. I got all sweaty when we gathered in the auditorium to recognize the winners. I didn't even get an honorable mention. Attending various writing meetings over the next two days, I was humbled. I realized I had a long way to go and a lot to learn.

As the conference ended, I climbed in my trusty Camry and headed west, leaving behind those people who didn't recognize genius. My destination was the quaint but picturesque town of Cuchara, Colorado.

Renting a small mountain cabin, I planned to write for six days. That sounded like a lot of time to write and I hoped to start and finish two books. I'm always amazed at how I can be so insecure and so grandiose at the same time.

I did *start* both books that week. I also drank a lot of good coffee and wore my colorful flannel shirts around town. I love my home state of Texas, but to escape the blazing heat and enjoy the cool mountain air and afternoon showers of the Rockies, well that's a little bit of heaven, and something to write home about. So I did have a great week, and I learned full-time writing is not so easy and not so glamorous.

While I had started several chapters of this, book, I was still trying to figure out exactly what I wanted to do and how to organize it. I decided I needed to read some more and think some more and ask God to guide me. Hence, I set it aside and just focused on my ADHD book. Get it? I focused on my ADHD book.

Six months later I felt like I had clearer path for this book. A couple of people, who knew about the potential book, encouraged me to start working on it again. Every other week I would take a chapter to my Christian Writers group for critique. I struggled with using active verbs and staying in the right tense. I was also wordy and redundant. Did I already say that?

In the Middle of the Lake

Donald Miller, in *A Million Miles in a Thousand Years: How I Learned to Live a Better Story*, shares about a canoe trip he took across a large lake. He'd been dreaming about this challenging canoe trip for a long time. His excitement peaked as he pushed off the shore and began to paddle. Looking back at the shore, he could tell he was he was moving fast. But once in the middle of this large lake, though he was steadily paddling, he couldn't tell if he was making any progress at all. The other side seemed to be staying the same size. His point was, even in exciting projects, there are hard times where you just have to plug away, even if you feel like you're not getting anywhere.

I can relate to that with my book. Certainly, that had been my experience building the tree house. While it was fun and exciting, it was hard work and there were times I became discouraged and wondered if I would ever finish. But I'm learning God likes us to be in the present, enjoying the moment. We often get way out ahead of ourselves and pay the price with worry and discouragement.

Responsibility and Joy

I am betting that you have a lost part. Something you loved and were good at, but lost in the busy-ness of life. Take time to reflect if there is something you once enjoyed, but have lost. Ask God to help you recall any lost parts. I think you will find it satisfying and enriching to reclaim this part. It may take some time, as it did for me, but it will be worth it. I suspect the part you are reclaiming, was part of your original design. You have the responsibility (parent ego state) and the joy (free child ego state) of developing it. Maybe there is not time in your life-stage now to fully develop your lost part, but there is probably a way to start. Just enjoy starting. If it is a passion for you, more time will probably come later.

Questions for Reflection and Discussion

- In reading this chapter, did you think of something you once enjoyed and perhaps excelled, but for some reason you set it aside for years? Can you explain why you set it aside?

- Would it be okay if you picked up this "lost part" of you and began to enjoy it and develop it again?

- Or maybe there is another part of you for which you have some passion and longing. Is now the time to develop that part? If so, how would you start?

- What is the main thing inside of you that keeps you from doing something you really want to do?

Chapter 10
Nine Versions of Ego

More Than a Type Test

The Enneagram is a system for psychological and spiritual growth. You are identified by a number, 1 through 9, based on your personality. While the Myers-Briggs is about normal personality types, the Enneagram is more than just a type test; it is *a tool for deep psychological understanding and spiritual transformation.*

My Enneagram Story

I encountered the Enneagram twenty years ago. It wasn't as developed then and I couldn't find a test. I read summaries of the nine types. Some I discarded immediately as "not me." The 6 type sounded like me. Sixes' are loyal and dependable. They struggle with anxiety, worry, and insecurity and can have some dependency issues. That all sounded like me. Since I was already aware of these tendencies and had been in therapy several times, I didn't find the 6 material particularly enlightening.

Several years passed. One day a counselor friend, who used the Enneagram in her practice, challenged me to read the Type 4. She knew me well and thought it might fit me better than the Type 6. By this time *The Wisdom of the Enneagram,* by Riso and Hudson, had been published, and the whole system was better developed. As I read about the Type 4, I realized that possibly I had miss-typed myself as a Type 6 years earlier. Reading about the Three Centers helped me clarify the difference between a 6, in the Thinking Center, and 4, in the Feeling Center. Below is a brief introduction to the Three Centers. Which Center best describes you?

The Three Centers

The Triad, three-parts, consists of three components of the psyche. Each Triad describes a cluster of issues and coping mechanisms. These concepts come from *The Wisdom of the Enneagram*.

Instinctive (Types 8, 9, 1)	Resist reality. Struggle with aggression and repression. Underlying rage.
Thinking (Types 5, 6, 7)	Feel a lack of support. Strive for safety and security. Underlying fear.
Feeling (Types 2, 3, 4)	Concerned with self-image. Think their False Self is who they really are. Underlying shame. (Riso, The Wisdom of the Enneagram, 1999, p. 51)

Identifying with the Feeling Triad narrowed me down to either a Helper (2), an Achiever (3), or an Individualist (4). With further reading, I had to agree with my counselor friend, Type 4 fit me.

This Type 4 insight made a real difference in my life: undeveloped 4s tend to stay stuck in fantasies about: (1) what they could do some day (future focus), or (2) self-incriminations about their failures, feeling shame (past focus). Wow! This fit for me.

Fortunately, *The Wisdom of the Enneagram* didn't stop with this grim analysis. It explained 4s can feel competent and confident when they get out of fantasy (avoidance) and focus on tangible projects that they follow through to completion. I took that advice and applied it to my passion for carpentry. The fantasy of building a cabin someday turned into the reality of a two-level treehouse twenty-five feet in the trees. I enjoyed the creative work immensely, and I felt I had really accomplished something. Over the last three years, I have made a commitment to writing and I am in the process of finishing my first book. The helpful advice for the Type 4: Focus on one project at a time, and bring it to completion.

There is a similar life-changing analysis and instruction for each Enneagram type.

The Nine Types

The nine personalities of the Enneagram are given different names by different Enneagram authors:

AUTHORS RISO & HUDSON	AUTHOR HELEN PALMER
1. The Reformer	The Perfectionist
2. The Helper	The Giver
3. The Achiever	The Performer
4. The Individualist	The Tragic Romantic
5. The Investigator	The Observer
6. The Loyalist	The Loyal Skeptic
7. The Enthusiast	The Epicure
8. The Challenger	The Protector
9. The Peacemaker (Riso, The Wisdom of the Enneagram, 1999)	The Mediator (Palmer, 1991)

Strengths of Each Type

One, The Reformer: Moral, disciplined, they want to improve the world, and they are good at getting things done.

Two, The Helper: Warm, sensitive to others, they enjoy helping family and friends.

Three, The Performer: Confident, highly-driven, and image conscious.

Four, The Individualist: Sensitive, self-absorbed, they desire to find themselves and create something of beauty or meaning for others.

Five, The Investigator: Curious and insightful, they seek to understand complex things of the world.

Six, The Loyalist: Security oriented with sense of humor, they are loyal and dependable.

Seven, The Enthusiast: Outgoing, high-energy, optimistic, they seek to find new experiences.

Eight, The Challenger: Self-confident, strong, protective, they charge ahead to accomplish goals.

Nine, The Peacemaker: Laid-back, peace-loving, they take life as it comes and adapt to it, trying to avoid conflict.

Finding Your Enneagram Type

Please go to the website below. You can take a short, free version of their test or you can take their official test for only $10.
http://www.enneagraminstitute.com/Tests_Battery.asp#FreeShortTests

A version of the Enneagram may be found, along with other tests, on the Similar Minds website. These tests are free.
http://www.similarminds.com

Explore

Your results will get you into the ballpark of your type. Then you can begin to read some of the descriptions until you feel more certain about your type. There are descriptions of each type by various Enneagram authors. To find these do a web search by entering your Enneagram type, for example, enter: Enneagram Type 2.

Take Enneagram with a Friend, Discuss Results

It can be helpful to involve someone who knows you well and get their feedback on which type sounds like you. Sometimes we don't see our own type clearly because we can't be totally objective about ourselves. I probably rejected my own type initially because I didn't like some of what it said. Several years later I realized those characteristics I disowned were actually there. We each have a way we like to see ourselves, but we have blind spots. Again, it is beneficial and fun to explore your Enneagram type with a couple of friends who are also seeking to know themselves.

This is Only an Introduction

I want to emphasize that reading this chapter will not tell you everything you need to know about the Enneagram for your growth. My goal to whet your appetite for further study because it is such a great tool for your psychological and spiritual growth.

Three Revealing Concepts of the Enneagram

- Direction of Disintegration (Stress)
- Direction of Integration (Growth)

- Levels of Development

Direction of Disintegration (Stress)

Each Enneagram type has healthy and unhealthy behaviors. When you experience stress, your Enneagram type tends to go toward the unhealthy levels of one of the other eight types. For example, when I feel stressed or anxious as a Type 4, my direction of disintegration is Type 2, The Helper. I will stop being my intuitive, creative self and become overly helpful or clingy.

Let's look at the Direction of Disintegration for each Type:

UNDER STRESS	BEHAVIOR
1's go to the unhealthy 4	Behave moody, illogical
2's go to the unhealthy 8	Behave dominating, bossy
3's go to the unhealthy 9	Behave apathetic, low motivation
4's go to the unhealthy 2	Behave overly helpful, dependent
5's go to the unhealthy 7	Behave impulsive, scattered
6's go to the unhealthy 3	Behave competitive, superior
7's go to the unhealthy 1	Behave critical, picky
8's go to the unhealthy 5	Behave secretive, anxious
9's go to the unhealthy 6	Behave worried, fearful (Riso, The Wisdom of the Enneagram, 1999, pp. 88-90)

As you become more aware of what you do when you are stressed, you can deal with your anxiety and not have to act out the unhealthy behavior of another type.

But the Enneagram doesn't stop there; it also directs you toward a growth direction for your particular type.

Direction of Integration (Growth)

The good news is each type also has a Direction of Integration. This is a real gift of the Enneagram.

IF GROWING	NEW BEHAVIOR
1's go to the healthy 7	Become playful, allow pleasure, joyful
2's go to the healthy 4	More aware of feelings and needs
3's go to the healthy 6	Able to commit to others
4's go to the healthy 1	Operate from principles and take Action
5's go to the healthy 8	Move into their body and instincts for grounding in reality
6's go to the healthy 9	More aware of their bodies in the moment, give their head a rest
7's go to the healthy 5	Better able to sit with their observations and experiences
8's go to the healthy 2	Become able to open their heart to others
9's go to the healthy 3	Take action and begin to feel feel valuable (Riso, The Wisdom of the Enneagram, 1999, pp. 91-94)

Awareness of these directions of disintegration and integration helps us know ourselves more deeply. It also gives us insight into those we live with and work with. As a therapist, it equips me help people better because I understand them, and I know where they need to head for growth. But that's not all.

Levels of Development

Don Richard Riso of The Enneagram Institute researched and created the nine Levels of Development as gauges of health. He began with three levels: healthy, average, and unhealthy. This took the Enneagram from just another horizontal "type system" to a type system with a vertical dimension. Now we can talk of a Type 3 who is healthy, average, or unhealthy in his level of development. We can now understand why two Type 8's can look so different. One is an unhealthy or average health 8, and one is a healthy 8. Later, Riso added three levels within each of the three levels. See below. This applies to each of the nine types.

Healthy	1	Our type is not limiting us much: gratitude, peace, and intimacy with God
	2	Actualized, high-functioning
	3	
Average	4	With transformational work, we can move up
	5	Most people live around levels 4, 5, or 6
	6	Under stress, we can temporarily drop one or two levels
Unhealthy	7	
	8	Pathological, low-functioning
	9	Over-identified and caught up in our type

(Riso, The Wisdom of the Enneagram, 1999, pp. 75-88)

To see the level of development specific to your type, get a copy of *The Wisdom of the Enneagram.* You may also find the Levels of Development on their website.

www.enneagraminstitute.com

Two Ways to Check Your Growth

- Look at your type's Direction of Integration and Direction of Disintegration. Are you going in a good direction for yourself or a negative direction?

- Look at the Level of Development for your type. Are you moving up or down or staying the same?

Spiritual Transformation and Death

In the spring of 2012 I attended a three-day Enneagram workshop north of Albuquerque. Our setting was the new home of one of the leaders. The spacious home had an adobe look with beautiful southwestern décor. It was an intimate workshop with two leaders and seven participants. From the living room, we looked out to the rugged New Mexico landscape with a river and mountains in the distance.

During introductions, we learned each person's type and level of experience with the Enneagram. The only type 4 there, I felt special and was sure the leaders would be impressed to hear they had a creative 4 in the group. Actually, they didn't seem impressed.

I soon picked up that it's not good to be too identified and too caught up in your type. In fact, it was a goal of the workshop that each Enneagram type would see their path of moving up the Levels of Development – moving away from their familiar box. The instructors talked of letting go of one's story about who they were. Here I was, naively excited to be a wonderful 4, and they were talking about letting go of this creative identity with which I had become so enamored.

But what about my pet projects? My carpentry, my writing – the new and wonderful creative me? Isn't this part of my True Self?

What I learned in that workshop and over the next few months, is that while these pet projects fit me and offered a chance for me to develop, they are *to be held lightly*. My true calling is to make time for God and get to know who He really is. My calling is to not just ask for God's stamp of support on my projects, but to be still and listen to Him. It's not about me and the cool things I can do in my quest to be good and to be great. It's about God. Only God is Good. Only God is Great. He alone has true wisdom. He alone is sovereign. In getting to know Him, I can align with Him. Thy kingdom come, Thy will be done.

Don't Put Me in A Box

In their excellent book, *The Wisdom of the Enneagram*, Riso and Hudson say that as humans, "we have fallen asleep to our true nature." This is because our personality (ego) tends to dominate and run things. The Enneagram can remind us of our spiritual nature by providing highly specific insights into our psychological and spiritual makeup. The Enneagram also helps us by giving us direction in which to work, but only as long as we remember that it is not telling us who we are, but how we have limited who we are.

Remember, the Enneagram does not put us in a box, it shows us the box we are already in – and helps us find the way out.

As noted above, I initially missed the Enneagram's main point, which is: as we become more aware and attentive to our soul, then God helps us grow beyond our old ego-driven way of living life.

The Apostle Paul put it this way,

> [Not in your own strength] for it is God who is all the while effectively at work in you [energizing and creating in you the power and desire], both to will and to work for His good pleasure and satisfaction and delight. (Philippians 2:13, *Amplified Bible*)

> That energy is God's energy, an energy deep within you, God himself willing and working at what will give him the most pleasure. (Philippians 2:13b, *The Message*)

Nine Versions of Ego Life

The Enneagram describes nine versions of ego life. We can't totally do away with our version, whichever of the nine we may be, but we can be less limited by it. In spiritual maturity we can, move fluidly among the other eight versions as the situation calls for it. We have the potential, as we know God and trust our security to Him, to live out of our box!

Want to Make God Smile? Tell Him Your Plans

Joseph saw great things for his life. God's plan involved years of slavery and imprisonment before He elevated Joseph to great power in Egypt – to save Israel from starvation.

Moses wanted a safe, non-speaking life as a shepherd. God's plan put Moses in the face of the mighty Pharaoh, telling him to let the Israelites leave Egypt.

Jonah hated the people of Nineveh and refused God's instruction to warn them of their destruction. God's plan stuffed Jonah in the belly of a great fish for three days to motivate him to preach to the Ninevites.

Peter wanted to protect Jesus and keep him alive. God's plan was to humble Peter who, within hours, denied Christ three times. God then empowered the broken Peter with the Holy Spirit. He became a key leader in the early church.

Saul (Paul) had a zealous plan to rid the world of Christians. God's dramatic plan called for Saul's blinding and renaming. Later, relying on Christ, Paul became the first missionary to the Gentile world.

Even Jesus questioned the cup, but He chose to obey his Father. God's plan took Jesus through torture, even to death on a cross, so that man could be forgiven and brought into real life with God.

Review of Key Points

- The Enneagram is a tool to help you be more aware of your personality box – your version of ego – so you can begin to see your way out.

- When in the Average Level of Development or the Unhealthy Level of Development, you are caught up and locked rigidly into your personality.

- The Enneagram shines a revealing light on our version of ego. As we see the futility of our ego-driven life, God draws us to Him and we move to the Healthy Levels of Development (parallels the True Self). We begin to live more out of the soul/True Self as we find union with God.

- The Enneagram supports the biblical viewpoint that life is not about me, life is about knowing God and following Him.

For Further Study

The Wisdom of the Enneagram by Riso and Hudson.

Website: www.enneagraminstitute.com

The Enneagram: A Christian Perspective by Richard Rohr

www.lifeinthetrinity.com Workshops by Suzanne Stabile, a Master Teacher for the Enneagram. I also recommend her CDs and her DVD series for church groups.

Enneagram Testimonial

Lalla Shackelford

My first experience using the Enneagram was on an extended retreat with a group of eight friends who had known each other well for many years. As we talked briefly about how we scored, I was amazed at the accuracy of how the summaries revealed what I had observed to be true about my friends and myself.

It was this practical experience of the tool that captured my attention. Although there was much information on the history and development of the Enneagram, I focused on my type and kept finding information that resonated deep within me.

I was in a small group of women serious about our pursuit of Jesus and how to encourage one another along on the way. We began looking at the Enneagram together and it helped each of us tremendously to quickly learn so much about one another.

The clear definitions of basic fear, basic desire, and superego message got me started. Then the suggestion to "observe" these things in myself began working to be what I defined as good to deep conversations with Jesus about my observations, seeking his input. This of course opened me to knowing Him as He led me through Scripture, meditation, and contemplation related to the daily life experiences we considered.

The concepts of wings, disintegration/integration, and levels of development have become helpful over time. But most helpful to me is the daily Enneagram Thought I receive from the Enneagram Institute. These brief thoughts are reminders about my One type and suggest awareness for the day. These insights are always applicable to my day, reminding me how I am a One and how to release my ego's fixations on the negative aspects of self.

The Enneagram is not responsible for my spiritual growth, nor am I; it is a

---

gift of grace. But the Enneagram information has helped me become aware of my tendencies to resent the way things are and to want to fix them. As a result of that awareness and interactions with Jesus about it, I am letting go of my striving to control and instead surrendering to what he brings to my life, opening to his desires rather than to my own.

In relating to others, I have learned that our differences are much deeper than personality qualities. In both my personal and professional life I have found it helpful to be more aware of what type a person is and to research what can be helpful to that type's spiritual growth. I feel more comfortable coming along beside them in this way than using my old pattern of criticism and control. As I have learned how gentle and patient Jesus is in showing me areas of growth, I find I am more willing to take on those qualities with others. I can enjoy being a part or what Jesus is doing rather than pushing my own agenda based on my own desires.

When I am fortunate enough to share with someone how God has worked in my life, the first thing I emphasize is spending time with Him most every day, talking honestly with Him about everything in life. Someone who is willing to do this in community with one or more who also spend time with Jesus, will start to see their patterns of behavior. At that point the Enneagram can be a helpful tool to encourage spiritual growth.

The Enneagram is an easy tool to use but using it is not easy. It brings up painful realizations and confronts uncomfortable behavioral patterns, but it does so in the context of hope for change and a view of how that change might look.

Questions for Reflection and Discussion

- Was it uncomfortable to find your Enneagram type and read about your issues? Remember each type has issues. We can choose to avoid our issues or we can start to face our issues.

- Think about and share with a person you trust what a negative direction is for you. For help, look at your type's Direction of Disintegration.

- Think about and share with a person you trust what a positive direction is for your type. Look at the Direction of Integration for your type.

- "Therefore if any man be in Christ, he is a new creature: old things are passed away; behold, all things are becoming new." (2 Corinthians 5:17, KJV) Does this verse have any new meaning in light of the Enneagram perspective?

- Moving from an ego-run-life to a God-led-life is done in God's power? How is this accomplished? What is your role?

Part II: Knowing God

Introduction to Knowing God

Some may be puzzled by my change of direction. What does knowing God have to do with knowing yourself? Certainly, the larger, Knowing Yourself section of this book has standalone value. But for the person with a spiritual commitment, knowing God makes perfect sense. God designed and created us. He is all knowing so He knows us each intimately. Our very life comes from Him.

As Jesus began His ministry, he picked his disciples. He invited Philip to come and follow him. Philip then found Nathaniel and told him they had found the Messiah. When Jesus saw Nathaniel approaching, He commented, "Now here is a genuine son of Israel – a man of complete integrity."

Nathaniel asked, "How do you know about me?"

"I could see you under the fig tree before Philip found you."

Nathaniel then called him Rabbi and recognized Jesus as the Son of God. (John 1:43-49, NLT)

In the woman at the well story, Jesus offered a despised Samaritan woman living water. During their interaction, He let her know that He knew she had been with five husbands and now lived with another man. She made some reference to the Messiah coming some day with all the answers. He told her He was the Messiah. She then returned to her village and said,

"Come see a man who knew all about the things I did, who knows me inside and out. Do you think this could be the Messiah?"

Yes. Jesus knows each of us intimately. Better than we know ourselves.

Think of it this way, if you bought some great software that was specific to knowing yourself, for example "Understanding and Knowing Jane Doe," it would be additionally helpful to have access to the person who wrote the software. Fortunately customer support came with your software. You can call and consult with the developer who knows this Jane Doe software in and out.

If you believe God knows everything about you and if you want to know yourself, it makes sense that developing an intimate communication with God will greatly help you in your goal of knowing yourself.

And truth be told, the goal of knowing yourself is a necessary step toward the larger goal of being transformed. Some might think of it as developing the best version of yourself. But for Christians, we are being transformed into the image of Christ, which does end up being the very best version of ourselves. As St. Paul wrote to the Galatians:

> My little children, for whom I am again in the pain of childbirth until Christ is formed in you. (Galatians 4:19, NRSV)

To that end I offer three chapters and six stories in this Knowing God section:

Knowing God's Gift	Grace, His unconditional love
Knowing God's Will	His sovereign will. He is orchestrating our lives for good to accomplish His purposes
Knowing God's Desire	He wants us to spend time with Him, to be loved and changed by Him
Knowing God's Voice	Six stories of women and men who have pursued intimacy with God

Now we begin this section with Chapter 11, Knowing God's Gift.

Chapter 11

Knowing God's Gift

Welcome to Knowing God, the second part of our journey.

I believe knowing God has great relevance to knowing ourselves. After all, He created us and is intimately involved in our daily lives. He is our Heavenly Father and we are His children.

While the human mind can't fully comprehend God, He has revealed Himself. First, through creation, then through Abraham, and then through the Mosaic Law. And, more completely when He humbly became flesh. The God of the universe became human and walked and talked among us! The surprisingly quiet arrival of the longed-for Messiah. And finally He revealed Himself through the written record, the God-inspired Scriptures that spanned over four thousand years of God interacting with man. It is clear that God wanted us to know Him.

God's gift to us is often summed up and known as grace. And everybody wants a gift, don't they?

Kids Get So Excited

Kids count down the days until Christmas. With bright faces and excited speech, they corner you with what they hope to find under the tree. It's the gifts.

Picture an adult walking down the street. A strange man approaches and says he has a gift for him. In the blink of an eye his body tightens and his heart beats faster. He mutters, "No thanks," as quickly walks away.

What is the difference between the child's excitement and the adult's fear? The child trusts his parents and knows they give good gifts. The adult is wary the stranger is trying to hurt him or take advantage of him in some way. The savvy adult knows a stranger won't give you a free gift. There's a catch. Something that appears to be free can't be trusted. To get something of value, you have to pay for it.

It's been said, "Never look a gift horse in the mouth," but we do. If a friend surprises you with a gift, you might say, "What's the occasion?" There has to be a deserving reason like it's your birthday or you house-sat for them. Once we get out of childhood, we seem to become wary of the free gift.

Perhaps this discomfort is rooted in our childhoods. If we were good, we got a treat. If we made a mess, we had to clean it up. We worked hard, we got rewarded. We learned how the world worked. Smith Barney, a stock brokerage firm, made a slogan of it: "We make money the old-fashioned way. We *earn* it." It all made sense.

It all made sense until Jesus came along. He taught some radical things. He called out the religious elite, the Pharisees. Jesus called them hypocrites. He hung-out with the down-and-out screw-ups. He told them of God's love and forgiveness. This was highly offensive to the religious. After all, they felt they had received God's favor the old-fashioned way – they earned it. They were threatened by this uneducated carpenter's son who talked like He knew God. Jesus brought God's gift, God's grace right before their eyes. They walked away, smugly saying, "Don't need it. I'll earn my own salvation, thank you."

Jesus also said that "Anyone who doesn't receive the Kingdom of God like a child will never enter it." (Luke 18:17 NLT) Puzzling. But a little child is trusting. They will jump at a gift. They sense who really loves them, and they want to be with them.

What is this radical gift Jesus made possible? What is grace? Let's take a look.

Definition of Grace

In the language of the New Testament, the Greek word for grace is *charis*. The most frequent meaning of charis holds that God's blessings to man are graciously bestowed, freely given, and are not based on any merit.

Paul put it like this: "For by grace you have been saved through faith; and that not of yourselves, it is the gift of God." (Ephesians 2:8, NIV).

We are not saved by our goodness or our works. It is all God's grace.

My Story of Dis-Grace

Growing up in a Christian family, belief in Jesus and faith in God made sense. My parents believed in God and took us to church on Sundays. We prayed at family meals. Though they seldom talked about their faith, they quietly lived it. My parents taught me and showed me how to live. Being a good Christian seemed like a natural part of my upbringing.

The key Scripture for kids to memorize was John 3:16. We knew that God loved us so much that He sent His only Son to earth for us. If we believed this, we would have eternal life. And we knew that Jesus loved us enough to die for us. I can't say that I thought of it as a gift from God. I viewed it as God had done this for us, and now I was supposed to do something for Him: be good and tell others about Jesus. The focus became what I needed to do. Since He died for me, I felt I owed Him something.

I looked at the world through the lens given by my parents. I wanted to be good to please my parents, so naturally I wanted to be good to please God. I didn't want to disappoint them or stir up my dad's wrath, and I didn't want God angry with me.

My focus wasn't on God. My focus was on being good. And if I couldn't always be good, at least I could usually make it look like I was good. This was the emergence of my little pharisaical False Self. It led to self-righteousness and a fear of being found out.

The Day Grace Meant Something

Leap forward fifteen years. It was my first year of psychology graduate school, with Christian professors. Bill Counts, a young seminary professor, taught a biblical class which was part of our program. He knew many of us had come from legalistic churches where the Christian subculture becomes confused with biblical instruction, for example, no drinking, no dancing, and church attendance three times a week. Some conservative Christian churches made the above a standard for spirituality. Problem was, their standard did not come from the bible. It came from recent church subculture tradition. Counts taught from Scripture how Jesus often confronted the Pharisees on their self-righteousness. The Pharisees had tacked on another six hundred laws to go with the Ten Commandments. They were sticklers for keeping all these rules. They had become more focused on how good they looked on the outside (False Self) and ignored the condition of their hearts. Bill Counts' teaching helped me think and distinguish between practices in the Christian subculture and what the Bible actually taught. Necessary groundwork.

Counts then introduced us to a book by Pete Gillquist called *Love Is Now*. I brought this book home to my wife, and we both read it. Gillquist wrote that when God looks at us, He looks at us through Jesus and sees us as pure and holy. (Gilquist, 1970, pp. 47-49) As this sank in, it was a game-changer. Suddenly, there it was. The gift. His gift of grace. Our focus shifted from our efforts to please God and earn His favor, to seeing that we already had his approval. We already had his delight. There was no work or striving to add to that. Amazing. Grace. It was a sweet sound and still is.

Prior to this revelation, I had an obsessive-compulsive Christianity. I felt I should use all my time serving, studying the faith, or attending church services. When I wasn't doing one of these, I frequently felt guilty and worried that I wasn't doing enough to please God.

Also, I would think critically of other Christians who weren't as dedicated and sacrificing as myself. At that point I didn't know about Critical Parent messages (see Chapter 3), but these messages dominated my thinking. All the "should" that I should be doing as a Christian and all the "should" others should be doing. My head was a no-fun-zone, and my heart stockpiled bitterness.

A turning point came one June afternoon. My wife's friend from work invited us for a visit. She and her husband were nice folks and gracious to us. They were fortyish and in a second marriage with no children. They had a nice patio home in Orange County, southern California. We sat out on their sun-soaked patio and visited over some drinks. What struck me was how relaxed they appeared. It was after work, and they were just kicking back and sharing their patio and hospitality with us.

I contrasted this to my drivenness and worry. I realized the life I was living would not be a very attractive life to non-Christians. Secondly, I realized it wasn't attractive or satisfying to me. This OCD faith left me lacking two important feeling states: gratitude and peace. Bill Counts had anointed my head with grace the previous fall, but now it trickled down to my hard-working, tense heart. I thought, "If God loves me just as I am, and if there is nothing I could possibly do to gain His favor, then why do I have to push myself so hard and feel so guilty?" I had tried to earn my salvation.

Gradually, I began to thank God for all the good gifts He had provided rather than focus on my deficiencies.

I Fought the Law and the Law Won

At the right time in the story of the Israelites, God gave Moses the Ten Commandments. This became known as the Mosaic Law. Paul explained the purpose of the law in his letter to the Romans:

> God's law was given so that all people could see how sinful they were. But as people sinned more and more, God's wonderful grace became more abundant. (Romans 5:20, NLT)

The point of the law was to show us how totally incapable we were of being good, being moral. Failing to keep the law was to convince us that we needed a Messiah, a Savior who could restore our broken relationship with God.

If we had any illusion that we could keep the law, our illusion was blown away by Jesus' beautiful discourse known as the Sermon on the Mount:

> You have heard that our ancestors were told, 'You must not murder. If you commit murder, you are subject to judgment.' But I say, if you are even angry with someone, you are subject to judgment! (Matthew 5:21-22, NLT)

> You have heard the commandment that says, 'You must not commit adultery.' But I say, anyone who even looks at a woman

with lust has already committed adultery with her in his heart. (Matthew 5:27-28, NLT)

In Romans 7 Paul confesses his failure to keep the law:

> I have discovered this principle of life—that when I want to do what is right, I inevitably do what is wrong. I love God's law with all my heart. But there is another power within me that is at war with my mind. This power makes me a slave to the sin that is still within me. Oh, what a miserable person I am! Who will free me from this life that is dominated by sin and death? Thank God! The answer is in Jesus Christ our Lord. So you see how it is: In my mind I really want to obey God's law, but because of my sinful nature I am a slave to sin. So now there is no condemnation for those who belong to Christ Jesus. (Romans 7:21- 8:1, NLT)

Grace Flooded In

Pastor Chuck Swindoll, teaching on the superiority of grace (Romans 5:20), put it like this: "Where sin abounded, grace super-abounded. Where sin overflowed, grace flooded in." The Apostle John, introducing his gospel, wrote:

> For out of His (Jesus) fullness (abundance) we have all received [all had a share and we were all supplied with] one grace after another and spiritual blessing upon spiritual blessing and even favor upon favor and gift [heaped] upon gift. (John 1:16, Amplified)

As I recently listened to Dr. Swindoll's 2013 series on grace, I heard him admit he went through seminary without really understanding grace. I had to smile. Even the great teacher and pastor, Chuck Swindoll, didn't "get it" at first. I didn't feel so bad about my slowness. (Swindoll, 2013)

Sometimes grace strikes with dramatic force as Saul found out on the road to Damascus. Blinded by a brilliant light, he fell to the ground, confronted by the words of Jesus Himself. "Saul! Saul! Why do you persecute me?" (Acts 9:3, NLT) The leading persecutor of the church would persecute no more. Jesus blinded him so that he could see.

Saul saw the Light and became Paul, appointed missionary to the Gentiles. Forgiveness of the chief sinner. God's grace!

Law vs. Grace on the Big Screen

"Les Miserables," the 2012 musical based on Victor Hugo's French Revolution era novel, presented a dramatic contrast between the law and grace. Jean Valjean, played by Hugh Jackman, had served twenty years of hard labor for stealing a loaf of bread. Starved and bitter, he experienced grace from a kindly priest. He learned he has a soul. Valjean was humbled and changed forever. Russell Crow played Javert, a prison guard turned local police officer. He was a legalist to the letter of the law, driven to bring Jean Valjean to justice for violating his parole. "Les Miserables" fleshed out the gospel story of grace and redemption. It also showed the tragic end of the legalist who rejected grace. (Hooper, 2012)

Story of the Father's Love

The religious criticized Jesus for hanging out with sinners. Jesus responded with three parables, one of which is known as the Return of the Prodigal Son. The father's younger son demanded his inheritance early, which he then wasted in sinful living in a distant country. His loving father waits and longs for his return. This is where we pick up with the father's response to the son's return.

> So he returned home to his father. And while he was still a long way off, his father saw him coming. Filled with love and compassion, he ran to his son, embraced him, and kissed him. His son said to him, 'Father, I have sinned against both heaven and you, and I am no longer worthy of being called your son.' But his father said to the servants, 'Quick! Bring the finest robe in the house and put it on him. Get a ring for his finger and sandals for his feet. And kill the calf we have been fattening. We must celebrate with a feast, for this son of mine was dead and has now returned to life. He was lost, but now he is found.' So the party began. (Luke 15:20-24, NLT)

This is grace, joyfully offered to the rebellious son. What struck me is Jesus knew His Father intimately, and he created this story to communicate the loving heart of His Father.

Is There "A Catch" to God's Free Gift?

Some might argue that there is a catch to grace because God asks something of us. That is a good point, because Jesus did say, "Follow me." There are examples in Scripture where Jesus tested the motivation of those who sought him. He told the rich young ruler to sell his possessions and follow Him. The man went away because he was too attached to his wealth. He was too comfortable in his plush, False Self.

Do we follow Jesus out of duty to earn our salvation, or do we follow Jesus because we love Him and want to be with him? He doesn't call us to follow a set of rules. He calls us to follow a person. Think about a sports hero or entertainment star you may have admired or become enamored. You wanted to meet them. Talk with them. Get to know them better. Where they went, you wanted to go. It's that child-like desire within each of us to connect with someone we perceive as awesome.

When each disciple first met Jesus, He offered an invitation, in effect saying, "Drop what you are doing and come with me." They saw and felt something that was powerfully attractive. How could they not follow Him? My point is, if you've found in Jesus Christ what you have been longing for and needing your whole life, you want to follow Him. You feel this incredible gratitude. You follow. You help. You stay by His side.

Excerpt from Kenny's Story

Crisis and Grace

After eighteen years, Kenny's marriage fell apart.

I had two episodes of adultery, and my wife wanted out. I became depressed. Maybe I was already depressed. A couple of years before the marriage ended, my dad had committed suicide.

Kenny went through deep depression because of the loss of his marriage and the loss of his dad. He felt much shame about the adultery. He took advantage of counseling and was eventually referred to a church that had a 12 Step program, and he worked on sexual addiction. He felt accepted there despite exposing his sin. Kenny began coming to the church and made close relationships in a men's discipleship group.

He recalled one particular Sunday morning:

One of the first services I went to was a Body Life service where people stood up and shared. I shared I experienced the trauma of divorce. I started crying right there. David and Rob came up and gave me a hug. I will always remember that day, because it opened me up to what a family of Christians can be for each other. I talked about my worst problems and was shown a lot of grace.

While Kenny believes God was always active in his life, he admits he wasn't aware of it. He feels God allowed him to go through the divorce and tragic loss of his dad to help him come to terms with his sexual issues and emotional issues.

I had never had a positive view of myself or accepted myself. I didn't have a big ego because I had never been a jock or a good student. I did just enough to pass. I never had the confidence to believe I could do anything well. Realizing that God accepts me, despite what I think of myself or what others think, has been critical for how I feel about myself today.

One of the powerful experiences that helped Kenny see how God felt about him happened when his church invited author, Brennan Manning, to speak at the men's retreat. Manning talked about the prodigal son and how the father saw his son at a distance returning. Kenny shared:

The father ran to his son and kissed him and welcomed him. It didn't matter what he'd done. He didn't even ask what he'd done. The father celebrated his return. It helped me see that God had never turned away from me. I had turned away, and He waited for me to come back.

More of Kenny's story can be found in Part III: The Stories

Questions for Reflection and Discussion

- When did you realize being accepted and loved by God was not about being good, not something you earned? When did grace click with you? If in a discussion group, tell of when you really understood grace.

- How does it affect the way you go about the Christian life when you realize God's grace is a free gift?

- Did you ever get so excited about someone that you wanted to be with them all the time? Maybe it was your mom when you were little. Or a big brother or sister. Or a girlfriend or boyfriend. You loved them, maybe even worshipped them.

- Is it possible to feel that way - wanting to be with them all the time - about God the Father or Jesus? Have you? Do you? If not, do you wish you did feel that strongly? It's okay to be honest about where you are at this point. Sometimes we're scared to let ourselves feel that way — scared to get really attached. Our old ego may not think that is smart.

Chapter 12

Knowing God's Will

At seventeen I didn't "get grace" although I had walked the aisle to accept Jesus at age nine. About to be a high school senior, I was focused, almost obsessed, with finding God's will for my life. Finding God's will meant discovering what career He had for me. With my ego-plan to be good and to be great, I decided I should be a foreign missionary. Relieved to have "God's will" nailed down, I headed to a small Baptist college as a ministerial student.

In my freshman year of college I took the basic courses as well as Old Testament and New Testament Bible courses. While I enjoyed these classes and learned a lot, I slowly began to question if I was really called into the ministry. Becoming friends with other ministerial students, I learned that several of them had a specific experience of God calling them into the ministry. I didn't have such an experience. My decision to be a missionary was more a logical deduction: since I am serious about being a Christian, I should go into full-time ministry. I imagined that God would be more pleased with me if I went into something self-sacrificing – foreign missions work.

Early in my sophomore year, God graciously spoke to me one night in my dorm room. I didn't hear a voice, but I recall reading words in a textbook from a ministry class: "Many young people feel called into Christian ministry today because our churches have given the message that is what one should to do if they are serious about following Christ." Wow! It felt like that sentence, that truth was hitting me right between the eyes. This truth instantly freed me from that False Self-script. Within five minutes I was thinking about how much I liked my psychology class. I felt becoming a Christian counselor was a better fit for me. God wasn't drafting me into a mission career I didn't really want.

Why the Focus on God's Will and Sovereignty?

I believe Christians who know themselves better are in a good position to know God better. Since we are in the process of moving from an ego-run life to a God-led life, it makes sense to become more aware of His sovereignty and His will. As the scripture says:

> For my thoughts are not your thoughts, nor are your ways my ways, says the Lord. For as the heavens are higher than the earth, so are my ways higher than your ways and my thoughts than your thoughts. (Isaiah 55:8-9, (NRSV)

Sovereign Will

Allow me to zoom out for the big picture regarding God's will and sovereignty. Christian theology has taught that God's sovereignty has two parts: His sovereign will and His sovereign power.

Regarding His sovereign will, Deuteronomy 29:29 NRSV) says, "The secret things belong to the Lord our God, but the revealed things belong to us and to our children forever, to observe all the words of this law." Theologian Louis Berkof explained that God's revealed will is what we know from the Bible, that is, God's law and the gospel. God's secret will is not something we can know until it is completed. (Berkof, 1959, pp. 82-84)

At times we can reflect on past experiences and get a better idea of what God was doing. Sometimes insight comes many years later.

Understanding God's Will After the Fact

Looking back on my life, I believe I see times God led me and directed me. I imagine you can see the same in your life. Last week I dropped by a rehab hospital to visit with my best friend's Dad who recently broke his leg. Sam has been a rancher most of his life. Sam and Margaret raised their kids in a little country church not far from my childhood home. He is now ninety-two and quite lucid. I asked Sam if he believed in God's sovereignty.

"Yes, I believe God is in control."

"Can you say more about that?" I asked.

"Well, I know there were things I wanted that didn't work out. Looking back I can see that what God gave me was much better than what I had wanted."

"Any specific memories of God working things out for your good?"

"In high school I took typing as an elective course. I didn't think much about it. Then when I went to the service during WWII, they put me in personnel because I could type. I had a desk job during the war. Without that typing course, I would have been infantry and might have died in the war," Sam shared. It was clear he believed God saved his life and that typing course was a part of God's plan.

That's hindsight. Looking forward we don't know the specifics of our personal futures. These things are not for us to know. When Jesus was on earth, he taught of His second coming: "But about that day and hour no one knows, neither the angels of heaven, nor the Son but only the Father." (Matthew 24:36, NRSV)

Open Doors, Closed Doors: God's Will

I had the privilege many years ago to serve on the board for the Christian Association for Psychological Studies. Our executive director was Bob King. Bob was probably ten years older than most of us. A former Air Force pilot, he had become a counselor as a second career. He was a gentleman and an effective leader and manager.

After his first term as executive director, he applied to serve a second term. As the board, we were about to vote on it. Bob expressed that he would love to serve again, but that he would consider whatever we decided as God's will for him. That impressed me, and I've never forgotten his wisdom. Sometimes we go for something we want, but if the door closes, we accept that as God's will for that time. By the way, Bob was re-appointed for another term.

Omnipotence: The Other Part of God's Sovereignty

To say God has superpowers would be a gross understatement. This is the other aspect of God's sovereignty mentioned above. The Almighty has complete power to do His will. Berkhof, writing on God's omnipotence, put it this way, "It does mean that He can, by the mere exercise of His will, bring to pass whatsoever He has decided to accomplish, and that, if He so desired, He could do even more than that." (Berkof, 1959)

Sometimes thinking of God's omnipotence scares us. Who hasn't feared that God might take away a loved one in death. We fear the Lord because we believe He is all-powerful. There are numerous stories in the Old Testament of God judging a pagan people and even Israel by consuming them in His wrath. He is God. He can exercise justice when He chooses. We ask for His mercy, as well we should.

A familiar verse from Proverbs speaks to this point:

> The fear of the Lord is the beginning of wisdom, and the knowledge of the Holy One is insight. (Proverbs 9:10, NRSV)

In one of my favorite scenes at the end of "The Lion, The Witch, and the Wardrobe" movie, little Lucy talked with Mr. Tumnus. She expressed how much she wished to still be with Aslan. Aslan was the Lion who represented Christ. Mr. Tumnus reminds her,

> "You know, Aslan isn't a tame lion."

> "But He is good, isn't He?" asks Lucy.

> Mr. Tumnus nodded. (Adamson, 2005)

A comforting scripture about God's nature and plans is: "For surely I know the plans I have for you, says the Lord, plans for your welfare and not for harm, to give you a future with hope." (Jeremiah 29:11, NRSV)

If God is good, and if He has plans not to harm us, then can we trust Him? Can we believe He wants to give us what we need? This is what Jesus said,

> Is there anyone among you who, if your child asks for bread, will give a stone? Or if the child asks for a fish, will give a snake? If you then, who are evil, know how to give good gifts to your children, how much more will your Father in heaven give good things to those who ask him! (Matthew 7:9-11, NRSV)

God's Power for Us and in Us

Years ago I went to a seminar by Reformed theologian, R.C. Sproul. He expanded my understanding of the Holy Spirit. He taught on John 14:16, where Jesus promised the disciples that after He left them, He would send them the Comforter. Sproul said that the King James Bible translators took the Greek word *parakletos* and translated it Comforter. Unfortunately, Sproul added, it doesn't communicate accurately to us in the twenty-first century. The English translators used Latin musical phrase *cum forte*. Seen in sheet music, the musician knows to "play it with power." So when the English read, Comforter, they thought of power and strength. Prior to this I had an image of a motherly Spirit patting me on the back to comfort me. A Spirit coming with power certainly fits better the story of Pentecost in Acts. The frightened disciples were filled with the Spirit and spoke with a new boldness. (Sproul, 1012)

My point is, God infuses us with portions of His power through the Holy Spirit, who indwells Christians. His power is a gift. His power does not come against us, but it strengthens and emboldens us – for He is our Father, and we are His beloved children. Pretty cool. I'm glad I'm on God's side.

The Story of Joseph
A Most Incredible Story of God's Sovereignty

God woke me to a new appreciation of His sovereignty in the summer of 2011. My pastor, Chip Bell, taught a series on Joseph. He called the series "Life in the Bowl." I would call the title bathroom humor if it was funny, but he was tackling a somber question. How do we react when our life appears to be going down the toilet? After a bright beginning, Joseph's life seemed to be "in the bowl" for many years.

Jacob fathered ten sons before he had Joseph. The son of his old age, Joseph became his favorite. When Joseph was seventeen he was shepherding with his older brothers. He brought back a bad report to his father. The brothers began to hate Joseph. Later Joseph received "a coat of many colors" from his doting father. The older brothers had received no such special gift. They were jealous of Joseph. Their disdain grew stronger when Joseph freely informed them of two dreams which suggested someday his older brothers would bow down to him.

The Older Brothers Had All They Could Take

When Joseph was sent later to check on his brothers, they had all they could take. They threw Joseph in a desert cistern and planned to leave him to die. The extreme hate in their hearts had turned into attempted murder. They were getting rid of this cocky kid. One brother felt some guilt and noticed a caravan of traders headed to Egypt. He persuaded his other brothers to sell Joseph into slavery instead of leaving him to die. To cover their crime, they ripped Joseph's beautiful coat and covered it with the blood of a goat. They acted innocently as they took the blood-stained coat to their father.

"Father. We found this coat. Can you tell if it's Joseph's?"

"It is my son's coat. A wild beast has devoured him and torn him to pieces."

Jacob was devastated and remained deeply depressed for years. He knew he would never see his dearest son again.

Joseph spent the next thirteen years in Egypt, either as a slave or as a prisoner. He fell from the height of his father's favorite to the lowly position of a slave and a prisoner in a foreign country. In my pastor's terms, Joseph's life was in the bowl.

While we might understand the brothers' jealous feelings and resentment, their free will decision to get rid of him was a horrible sin. It was a sin against God, against Joseph, and against their father. It set up years of suffering and grief.

Young Joseph in Egypt

Try to imagine being shipped off as a slave to a foreign country with a different language. From age seventeen to thirty you are either a slave or a prisoner. You lose your freedom during the prime years of your life. That is what Joseph endured. Quite a fall.

But God's hand was on Joseph despite his slavery and imprisonment. God raised Joseph to prominence in his master's household. He was appointed manager of the other servants. When his master's wife tried to seduce the handsome young Joseph, He refused and ran from the house. She accused him of sexual assault and he was imprisoned. Before long God raised him to a manager role within the prison. Yet, despite this unfair loss of his freedom, Joseph maintained his faith in God. In prison he became known for dream interpretation, but he made it clear that the interpretations came from his God.

God Rescues Joseph from Prison

Now, some thirteen years after Joseph became a slave, the Pharaoh of Egypt had two disturbing dreams. He was told Joseph could interpret dreams. He pulled Joseph out of prison and asked if he could interpret his two dreams.

"No, I can't," said Joseph. "But my God can interpret your dreams."

Joseph told Pharaoh that the dreams meant there would be seven years of plentiful crops followed by seven years of drought and no crops. He advised Pharaoh that he should appoint someone to oversee the saving of grain during the seven good years, so they would have enough in storage to see them through the seven lean years. Pharaoh was thankful and impressed. He appointed Joseph to oversee the program and to actually be second in command in all of Egypt. Doesn't it seem odd that Pharaoh would put a young Jewish man, fresh out of prison, second in command? If God wants something, it's going to happen. It may not seem plausible to the rational mind.

Seven years later the drought was so widespread that Jacob and his family back in Canaan were running out of food. Jacob sent his sons to Egypt to purchase food.

Joseph's Brothers Go to Egypt

When the brothers arrived in Egypt, they were sent to Joseph. They didn't recognize their brother as the regal ruler, who spoke Egyptian. Joseph recognized them immediately and questioned them about their family back home. He also tested their character and asked them to go home and bring back the youngest brother, Benjamin. After these tests, the brothers feared they were in trouble. Then things took an unexpected turn.

Can you imagine the shock when this powerful Egyptian official dropped the charade and warmly spoke in Hebrew:

> Please come closer. I am Joseph, your brother, whom you sold into slavery in Egypt. But don't be upset, and don't be angry with yourselves for selling me to this place. It was God who sent me here ahead of you...to keep you and your families alive and to preserve many survivors. So it was God who sent me here, not you! And He is the one who made me an adviser to Pharaoh – the manager of his entire palace and the governor of all Egypt. (Genesis 45:4-8, NLT)

> Even though you intended to do harm to me, God intended it for good, in order to preserve a numerous people, as he is doing today. (Genesis 50:20, NRSV)

Joseph clearly saw his slavery, imprisonment, and rise to power as orchestrated by God to accomplish His will.

Now

During my pastor's series on Joseph, I started to wonder: Was he suggesting God still orchestrates our lives today – just like with Joseph? I'm reminded of a joke attributed to the Yankee baseball great, Yogi Berra. When someone asked him what time it was, he responded with the question, "You mean now?" As I listened to my pastor, I thought to myself, "You mean now?" That is exactly what my pastor was teaching about God. The Lord is sovereign, and He is working in the circumstances of our ordinary lives, to accomplish His amazing will – now!

Three Benefits of Acknowledging God's Sovereignty in My Life

- I'm motivated to spend more time with Him – listening to Him. I want to cooperate and be about His will, not my ego-led plan.

- I feel less stressed. I have an agenda for the day, but I hold it loosely. In my busyness, I don't want to miss what He is doing around me. God gives me peace, because it's not all about me. God is orchestrating things for His purposes. It feels much better to know He is in control.

- Each day is an adventure. When something "goes wrong," I consider the possibility that God is doing something. "For my thoughts are not your thoughts, neither are your ways my ways, declares the Lord." (Isaiah 55:8, ESV)

Excerpt from Charles' Story

From Ego-Led To God's Sovereignty

Charles' faith was mostly about going to heaven. He and his wife became faithful church attenders at an independent Bible Church. Having an engineering background, Charles said:

My focus was to read the Bible, so I would learn how God wanted me to live. I thought of it as an instructional manual on how to live my life wisely, so God would bless me and so that I would honor Him.

Just a few years into his career, Charles was in charge of a fifty million dollar building project. One of the contractors went bankrupt, and as it turned out, his bonding insurance was not active. The client suffered a million dollar loss and sued Charles' company for the money.

When I found out they were suing us, I was devastated. I remember sitting in my car, leaning over the steering wheel with tears streaming down his cheeks, "I felt like I had done my best...I had done everything right, yet I was sure I would get fired."

Charles recalled thinking: "God you're showing me that You can do whatever you want...Even when I do my best, I'm not in control of the outcome."

It turned out his company's insurance covered the loss, and his boss was supportive. Charles said, "Because it smoothed over, I went back to my usual behavior of trying to do everything right...acting like I was in control again. I acted as though nothing had happened."

Years later, after slowing down and making time with God, Charles contrasted the majority of his Christian life, with his current experience:

It makes me tearful that I was so hard-headed. I drove down the highway of life in control – ignoring the huge billboards from God on each side of the road. I was so focused on where I was going and what I thought God wanted me to do that I wasn't taking time to watch and listen to Him for direction. I was self-directed instead of God-led. I had trusted God for salvation but not for my life.

Charles says he still struggles with how to hear God.

My tendency is to want clear direction and to drive my way through life, but I think He just wants me to listen to Him and be available. I keep looking for hard answers, but he just wants me to let go and rest in Him.

More often now, I feel a peace, because He is in control. The outcome is not up to me. God is doing it. My job is to hang in there with Him. I still must do things as I follow, but I can trust in Him for the results.

Charles's story in full can be found in Part III: The Stories.

Questions for Reflection and Discussion

- What if God is more "hands on" than you ever imagined? What if He's not just up there watching, only getting involved when enough people lobby Him for what they want?

- Think about some of the hard experiences and suffering which Joseph, Daniel, Paul, and even Jesus endured. Think about the hard times and tragedies that knocked you to your knees. Could God have been orchestrating those? I don't pretend to understand His ways, but it's possible. What do you think? Remember our ego strategies are designed to help us avoid anxiety, but God is about our growth, our maturing. He's not a tame lion, but He is good.

- How much do you try to control your day to meet your goals and expectations? We become so zeroed in on our targets, we don't look for or notice what He is doing. Our habits can be hard to change. How do you think you could become more aware of what God might be doing? How would you feel if you began to hold your desires and expectations loosely – ready to let them go at any time?

- How do you get to a feeling of peace even in the midst of things not going well?

Chapter 13

Knowing God's Desire

If you had asked me ten years ago what God desires from us, I would have listed:

He desires that we believe in Him.

He desires that we trust Him.

He desires that we serve Him.

He desires that we tell others about Him.

These are good things, but could God desire one thing even more?

He Doesn't Desire Our Sacrifices

The first time I heard this Old Testament scripture, I was surprised. Hosea revealed what God wanted:

> I don't want your sacrifices – I want your love; I don't want your offerings – I want you to know me. Hosea 6:6(ESV)

This has also been the thrust of my pastor's teachings for the last three years: God wants us to pursue Him, to hang-out with Him and get to know Him. That's the main thing. It's not about how hard we work for Him or how much we sacrifice.

A Passage that Makes Me Laugh

In Isaiah 30, we learn how the Israelites were in fear of their surrounding enemies. Rather than look to God, their collective ego hatched a plan to form an alliance with powerful Egypt. Isaiah brings the word of the Lord to them:

> This is what the Sovereign Lord, the Holy One of Israel, says: 'Only in returning to me and resting in me will you be saved. In quietness and confidence is your strength.' But you would have none of it. You said, 'No, we will get our help from Egypt. They

will give us swift horses for riding into battle.' (Isaiah 30:15-16, NLT)

The Message translation puts that last verse this way: "We will ride off on fast horses." That cracks me up. It is so American, so human. Rather than come to God in quietness, we devise our own strategy that involves speed. We forget to consult God. As one who has tried to ride off on a fast horse many times, I just have to laugh at myself.

Our God Is Relational, Personal

Christians have a relational God. When a Pharisee lawyer asked Jesus to give the greatest commandment, Jesus said, "You shall love the Lord your God with all your heart and with all your soul and with all your mind. This is the great and first commandment. And a second is like it: You shall love your neighbor as yourself." (Matthew 22:37-39, ESV)

My old ego-driven life was all about pleasing somebody and achieving something impressive. Just hanging out with God sounded rather lazy. I was sure God would be more pleased with me if I worked really hard for Him. Isn't that the way you achieve and get ahead? What kind of God wants me to sit and be still?

Maybe I had some misconceptions about God and His desire. You think? Maybe I didn't know God as well as I thought.

What We Desire

Since we are created in God's image, our human nature and desires should give us some clues about what God desires. What do babies want? They want their mothers. What do three year olds want you to do? They want you to play with them. What do teenagers usually want? They want to hang-out with their peers. What do we want when we fall in love? We want to be with the one we love. What do we want when we're old? We want our family and friends to come visit us.

We are relational creatures created in the image of God. Jesus Calling author, Sarah Young, writes a devotional as though Jesus were talking:

Do not feel guilty about taking time to be in My Presence. You are simply responding to the tugs of divinity within you. I made you in My image, and I hid heaven in your heart. Your yearning for Me is a form of homesickness: longing for your true home in heaven. (Young, 2004, p. 211)

And as we desire God in our deepest part, God desires to be with us, His children. He desires us to know Him and love Him. And as the Good Father, He delights in pouring out His love on us.

I know it's a little surprising, since He is running the universe.

God is relational. He desires to spend time with us, and He desires that we get to know Him and love him. How do we begin this?

Advice from a Spiritual Director

In my busyness, I related to Pastor John Ortberg's story from his book on spiritual disciplines, *The Life You've Always Wanted*. He had scheduled mentoring time with noted author and spiritual director, Dallas Willard. Ortberg asked Willard what was important in spending time with God and becoming intimate with Him. Willard said, "Ruthlessly eliminate hurry from your life." Ortberg hurriedly wrote that down, and asked Willard "What else?" The sage replied, "That's it." (Ortberg, 2002)

This is not easily done, living in an "instant" culture. Remember the twenty second TV commercial of a young man in a suit asking questions to a group of six year olds? In the ad for AT&T Internet service, he always ended with the wisdom, "Faster is better."

Apparently with God, faster is not better. Slower, quieter is better. How can we ever expect to hear God if we are moving at warp speed? Or if we are bombarded with noise? For years if I was by myself, I had the TV or radio on. Silence made me anxious. My thoughts would go to the negative, to the critical. No wonder I kept going fast and creating noise.

I now believe we can have conversations with God and get to know Him, but we must commit to making time for that. It takes time. Lots of time over months and years. But if we never start, we will never get there.

Have You Put in Your Ten Thousand Hours?

I enjoyed Malcolm Gladwell's book, *Outliers*, a study of how circumstances and upbringing may or may not lead to success. Gladwell made the observation that most accomplished people have put in at least ten thousand hours honing their skills. It might be a musician, an athlete, a professor, but if they're successful, they've put in their ten thousand hours. (Gladwell, 2012)

The ten-thousand-hour concept caused me to ponder: What would result if we were to put in ten thousand hours hanging out with God? At one hour a day, that would take about twenty-seven years. I also did the math that if the disciples hung out with Jesus for nine or ten hours a day, they would have gotten their ten thousand hours in three years.

My point is the same as Gladwell, it takes time to become accomplished at doing anything well. Of course, to know someone as immense and intelligent and complex as the God of the universe would obviously take some time, especially considering our intellectual and spiritual limitations. It is certainly a gift of great grace to have the opportunity to get to know Him. Jesus said that no one comes to the Father unless the Father draws him.

Fortunately, we don't have to put in ten thousand hours before we begin to hear from God.

God Spoke to Me Twice One Weekend

About three years ago I took my pastor's challenge to make daily time for God. I persisted with this morning discipline for several months. On a Friday night I had a dream. I was at an outdoor Christian gathering of some sort. Billy Graham was standing nearby. Being up in years and moving slowly, he needed someone to help him across a busy street. I volunteered and he held onto my arm. As we walked across the street, I could see my wife sitting on the other side in the crowd. I thought to myself, "I hope she sees me walking with Billy Graham." Evidently my False Self is still alive and well in my dreams. Anyway, I successfully brought Rev. Graham to the other side. I expected him to start talking to somebody important, but he held to my shoulder, as he continued to chat. I felt a little awkward and amazed that he wanted to talk to me. When I woke up, I knew he represented God in my dream. The message was God did enjoy the early morning times when we just hung-out together.

Saturday and Sunday, we had kept our two grandchildren for a few hours. Before leaving Sunday afternoon, Asher, my five-year-old grandson, called me over to where he sat and said, "Grampa, I don't get to see you enough. Could you come over and see us every Thursday when Gramma comes?"

Reflecting on this several days later, I found myself suspecting that God was trying to say something to me. In the span of thirty-six hours, He came to me as a greatly respected, wise, spiritual giant, and as an innocent, open little boy. Both wanted time with me. I got it, and I cried. I began to believe that the God of the universe desired and enjoyed the time I spent with Him. Amazing.

God as a Child

God spoke to me through my five-year-old grandson, and it helped me to know Him in a new way. I considered that an aspect of God was his purity, and perhaps in some way, He was even child-like. I have this memory from six years ago. My wife and I arrived at our daughter's home for a visit. Little Asher, only eighteen months old then, played in the next room. When he saw us, he got so excited. He jumped around and tried to reach us as fast as he could. We loved it.

If you are a parent or grandparent, you know what it's like to have your child or grandchild become excited when you arrive. The stresses of the day melt away when that little one runs to you and embraces you. There is purity in the simplicity of just being together. Is this not a glimpse of God's desire to embrace us?

Maybe that's why Jesus, in the busyness of saving the world, said, "Let the little children come to me, for to such belongs the kingdom of heaven." (Matthew 19:14, ESV) Jesus knew what was important. It wasn't keeping on schedule or making an impressive presentation. It was being with people, even little people, one on one.

After all, wasn't it God's plan to come to us as a baby, as a child. The Father could have sent Jesus to appear as an adult, ready to do ministry. But no, God came to us as a child who had a holy desire for relationships. A child who developed and grew over time. Like us.

We are in his image, and we have deep desires for relationship. God, as Spirit, doesn't have human needs, but He does have a strong desire for relationship with us, His children. In our fallen, broken condition, it is hard for us to see how much He loves us and desires to be with us. I don't think we could handle it if we realized how much God loves us. So I guess He helps us see it over time. The fullness of His love is not to be fully realized until we are in a different, less fragile form.

If you have the gift or ability to sit with a child and just "be with them," you have a godly trait of delighting in them the way our Father delights in us. The same applies if you spend time with an elderly person. Though they might be sick or frail and unable to do much for you, you still enjoy their company.

What Did Jesus Say?

During his ministry, Jesus and the disciples stopped at Martha and Mary's home. Martha welcomed Him, then returned to the kitchen to prepare the meal. Mary stayed at Jesus' feet, listening to Him. After a while, Martha came in and complained that Mary wasn't helping her. Martha told Jesus to tell Mary to help her in the kitchen.

Jesus replied to her,

> Martha, Martha, you are worried and upset about many things, but few things are needed—or indeed only one. Mary has chosen what is better, and it will not be taken away from her. (Luke 10: 41-42, NIV)

Jesus commended Mary for wanting to hang out with Him and hear Him.

Excerpt from Ben's Story

An Intentional Pursuit Is the Key

138

Four years ago Ben faced the fact he was sixty pounds overweight. He knew he needed to change his approach to food and that he needed structure. Ben made a decision and commitment. He began Weight Watchers. He tracked everything he ate and stayed with their point system. It worked. He lost sixty pounds.

A year later, he realized he and his wife had too much debt and always struggled financially. He decided to study Dave Ramsey's material from Financial Peace University. They followed his recommendations closely, and it worked. They got their debt under control and lived within their budget.

Ben said these two successes amazed him. Both changes came about with an intentional pursuit.

> My pastor had been encouraging us to spend time with God. He invited me to attend a weekly pursuit group with a few men. We each committed to spending time with God, talking and listening. We would journal and meet once a week to discuss our relationship with Christ.

Ben explained that this intentional pursuit of God has helped him experience God as much more personal. He said,

> It's like if I heard President Obama on TV ask people to donate to a good cause. I might consider it, but I'd probably not get around to doing it. But if the President knocked on my door and asked me to donate, I would probably do what he asked.

For more of Ben's story, see Part III: The Stories.

Is It Even Possible to Hear God's Voice? Really.

Getting to know God and hearing His voice start with slowing down and making time for Him.

Peter Lord in his book, *Hearing God*, tells the story of hosting a backyard party for his daughter who was in graduate school. She had several friends over. Lord noticed one man standing by himself in a remote area of the garden. He walked over and asked the young man if he needed anything. (Lord, 1988)

The young man said he was just listening to crickets. He explained further that he studied entomology, and he'd been doing research on crickets. He informed Lord that so far he'd heard eighteen varieties of crickets in the garden. (Lord, 1988, p. 27)

Lord had only heard one kind of cricket, or so he thought.

Lord was amazed the young man's hearing had become finely trained to distinguish different kinds of crickets. And I doubt the young man had reached his ten thousand hours.

Lord goes on to say, as we spend more time with God, His voice becomes clearer to us. It is more often that still, small voice rather than an audible voice.

When we spend quiet time with God and listen for His voice, thoughts come to our mind. Are these from God? Satan? Or could these thoughts be our ego?

Remember, our ego developed in childhood to help us solve problems and function as well as possible. The ego is our best human strategy. We each have our own version of ego, like the nine personalities of the Enneagram. So when we try to listen to God, we can expect our own ego-thinking will be one of the voices we hear. Distinguishing between God, Satan, and our own ego is the challenge. See why it's important for us to know ourselves.

Can We Trust It's God's Voice?

Christian psychologist and author, Gary Moon, gave us practical guidelines for hearing God's voice in his book, *Falling for God*. Moon names three stations from which we receive signals:

* WGOD

* WSIN

* WSLF (self) (Moon, 2009, p. 77)

Moon says WGOD is a little harder to tune into but once you find it, it has a loving, merciful tone, more what you would hear from the Good Shepherd. In contrast WSIN blares and is easy to pick up. It is hard to tune out.

Both Moon and Peter Lord draw distinctions between God's and Satan's voice. Here are three distinctions:

GOD'S VOICE	SATAN'S VOICE
Loving, affirming	Condemning, accusing
Consistent with scripture, God's overall teaching	More consistent with the world's values, human solutions.
Effect is encouragement, peace, love.	Effect is discouragement, worry, anger.
	(Lord, 1988)

As we learned earlier in this book, our version of ego has its own voice. Moon, going with the radio station metaphor, calls this WSLF. This is the third voice in our heads, actually the most familiar voice. Think of your Enneagram type. It's the way you think, the way you cope, your mode of operating. Maybe it's not necessarily bad, but it is distinguishable from the way God/The Good Shepherd talks to us and the way Satan accuses and discourages us. Maybe we can't totally delete our old ego's programming, but we can recognize it, and learn to differentiate it from God and Satan.

In conclusion, as impossible as it sounds, the Lord of the Universe loves it when we come to spend time with Him. We bring Him our burdens and He loves on us. In true gratitude, we thank Him and worship Him. As we learn to sit still and listen, we learn to hear His voice or sense His leading. These times are special gifts of grace.

Excerpt from Teresa's Story – Pursuing God

Although Teresa had tried quiet-time devotions, trying to connect with God through a devotion book or Bible study, she couldn't stick with it and it didn't connect her to God. Yet, now she found herself in a place in life where her sense of control was challenged.

My life philosophy was, if you try hard enough, if you put your mind to it, you can do anything. That was being challenged in a big way, and I was failing.

What I began to see and feel and hear God continually saying to me was one simple phrase, "Let me do it. Let me change you." All I did was have a deep longing desire to grow my relationship with God. I wanted to let God be in charge of me. So I started praying – even at times crying out for God to help me.

All of this Teresa chronicled in her journal. She found that when she honestly cried out to God, He gave her truth.

Teresa also realized that she could no longer "work" for her redemption. She had to lay down her self-pride, "can-do-good" attitude at Jesus' feet, admitting that only Jesus transforms.

Next came confessions from her youth. Rocky parts of her teen and young adult years revealed a longing to be good, but rebellious behavior emerged instead. "I knew this about myself, but I had never been able to truly look at it and feel it without running from the pain that was hidden and buried deep behind closed doors."

Teresa recalled that more memories and confessions followed for the next days. "I came to an overwhelmingly deep realization of how Jesus had pursued me across all those years, through all that rebellion. My rebellion wasn't bigger than his love for me."

Her confessions brought healing. Even now, over two years later, it brings a flood of tears. "Jesus was helping me know myself more, so I would know him more and trust him more. He loves me, not who I think I need to be. Isn't Jesus sweet?"

More of Teresa's story can be found in Part II: The Stories.

Questions for Reflection and Discussion

- If you believe God's greatest desire is that you come and spend time with Him, how could this change the way you live your Christian life? What would you do less of?

- Are you aware of any fear about slowing down and creating more moments of sitting quietly? How can you deal with your fear?

- Consider the possibility that some of God's character is child-like. The purity, the desire, the playfulness. Is this possible? Can you come to Jesus in child-like desire and dependence?

- Like the entomology student who could discern the different sounds of twenty-three varieties of cricket, do you think with practice you can recognize God's still, small voice as opposed to the other voices in your head?

- How can knowing your own personality and your way of thinking and approaching life be an aid in distinguishing God's voice as different than your own?

Part III: The Stories

Introduction to the Stories

We have sought to know God better through the previous three chapters. Fresh off our study of God's gift, God's will, and God's desire, it's time to hear stories of Christian brothers and sisters who have pursued an intimate relationship with God. They have made time for God. They have talked to God. They have listened to God. And they've chronicled their experience through keeping, for the most part, a daily journal.

Before they pull back the curtain and bare their souls, I want to tell you that I have known each of these dear people for several years. They are people of integrity who have been committed Christians for many years. For most, however, spending daily time with God and keeping a journal is a recent commitment in their spiritual walk – for most, it's been over the last four years. I have changed their names so that they would feel free to share even intimate details of their journey. Here are the stories of six modern day pilgrims who have come to *Know God* in a deeper way. They are learning to hear His voice.

I deeply appreciate their vulnerability in sharing. Their stories flesh out this book's truths in a very personal and tangible way.

Ellen's Story

Spiritual Background

Ellen can't remember not being aware of God. She was the oldest and her parents always took the family to First Baptist. Ellen recalled church as a place she enjoyed and a place where she felt accepted.

One Sunday during the invitation time, Ellen had this strange experience. Physically, it felt like butterflies in her stomach, but she also had the sense she looked down on her body. After church she told her dad what had happened. He said it sounded like God might be calling her, and if she felt it again when at church, she could go down and tell the pastor she wanted to trust Christ. It happened again and she walked the aisle and made her profession. She was nine.

Ellen recalled being excited about her big decision.

"I wanted to tell people about it but I didn't know how."

Ellen recalled her subsequent experience as a young Christian: I knew I had started this relationship with God, but I never learned how it was to continue. So I just went to church, read my Bible, and tried to live by the rules. I didn't have guidance, but I was trying to connect to God in a deeper way. As an adolescent, I was cognizant that there should be something more. It seemed rather easy to live a good life, but I felt a lack in being able to talk with people about what was going on spiritually. Now I realize there was not much going on.

Major Crisis

Ellen's father died when she was nineteen. She recalled her reaction.

I had just recently married, and thirty-five days, later my Dad died. It was so sudden. I kept functioning, but I couldn't handle the feelings so I just disconnected from people. There was too much going on inside. Driving home from college one day I was praying. I told God how unfair this felt. At the same time I thought God must perceive fairness in a different way. I didn't try to talk to anyone about my feelings. I thought if I didn't know why this had happened, then no one would. Back then I thought I was already supposed to know things.

Three years later Ellen completed a masters' degree, but struggled months to find a job. She remembered feeling inadequate and that her life was not going anywhere. She tried to keep things under wrap. Ellen began to sleep more and lost motivation for the things she usually enjoyed. Her husband suggested she might be depressed and it would be good for her to do some therapy.

Breakthrough

Being able to talk with a Christian therapist was just what Ellen needed.

It was a wonderful thing for me. It led to a major change in my spiritual life. In therapy I got to talk honestly, and I was taught how to deal with my feelings. The whole emotional world was just foreign to me. To learn a language for feelings was huge. I had been so achievement oriented. I realized I didn't understand God so much; I had just substituted Dad for God. Then Dad was suddenly gone.

One night after a therapy session, Ellen had a dramatic encounter:

I was driving home and it was quite dark. I had the perception there was light in my car. This was a wonderful, cathartic experience where I felt God's presence. I was thanking Him for releasing my feelings of anger, fear, and disappointment. I felt God really loved me and was pleased with me, and it wasn't because I was performing.

Ellen credits her therapy and this experience with God as launching her into the ability to deeply connect with people. For the first time, she realized that people had an inner emotional life that was important.

Spiritual Wilderness

Regarding spiritual growth, Ellen remembered dabbling in bible studies and trying to spend time with God. Looking back she realizes she didn't have the spiritual tools, and she didn't connect with a female mentor. The churches she attended were not that aware of spiritual direction or spiritual formation in the 1980's. Those who yearned for a deeper spiritual connection usually wandered in the wilderness with few tools or guidance.

A step in the right direction was Ellen's participation in a small group of Christian wives. They supported one another in the stresses of being wives and mothers. They also read and discussed Christian books such as Sue Monk Kidd's two books, *God's Joyful Surprise* and *When the Heart Waits*. These women searched for a more meaningful faith that spoke to their real struggles. They had done Bible studies before in which people had stayed on an intellectual level.

Practicing God's Presence

As Ellen began her forty's, there was a new wind blowing across evangelical Christianity. It may have started with Richard Foster's book, *Celebration of Discipline*. A close friend of Ellen's suggested they study a book called *The Devotional Classics*. It was a treasure of writings by key saints who over the centuries had sought intimacy with God. Ellen really enjoyed the study of how these Christians connected with God.

The *Devotional Classics* book introduced her to Brother Lawrence's book, *Practicing the Presence*. He taught the habit of focusing on God no matter what you're doing. Even washing dishes could be an act of worship and connection. It helped her see that God was in everything and that for the follower of Christ, there was no distinction between the sacred and the secular.

Sometime later, Ellen learned that a Christian counselor she had known for years had retrained as a spiritual director. Ellen had finally found a spiritual mentor. An example of one of the spiritual practices, she learned is lectio divina where one reads a short passage then invites God to speak to them through a several step process.

Spiritual direction became a process through which Ellen developed other mentors, women who were practiced in accompanying those on spiritual journey and offering information, tools and practice for growth.

Cancer: How Could This Happen?

In her mid 50's, Ellen was diagnosed with cancer. She remembers her shock,

> I thought I was doing all this stuff to be healthy, eating well and exercising, yet here I was with cancer. What's that about, God? Also, I felt like I'd failed — I must have done something wrong with my health or I wouldn't have cancer. I was still trying to control it, and not letting God be at work. I gradually accepted it, and allowed God to be present with me in it.

Ellen recalled a specific memory of connecting with God during this ordeal:

> I was going through a medical procedure where I was asked to lie on my left side. As I did, my arm outstretched with palm out. It reminded me of the Michelangelo painting of man reaching up and God reaching down. I used the technique of active imagination to practice the presence of Jesus. I offered that as an image for God to take may hand. Letting him comfort me and be with me during that procedure.

Journaling

Ellen doesn't remember when she began journaling but she has some journals from many years ago. Exposure to the writings of Gary Moon, who wrote *Falling for God*, spoke to Ellen about seeking God and hearing God.

A wonderful gift was placed in front of Ellen when her pastor returned from sabbatical with a new message. Through his ministry burnout, God had led him to see that our number one calling was to connect with God and listen to Him. Ellen explained why her pastor's new emphasis was such a gift: I was excited because he began in-depth teachings in all these things I had been circling around for years. It was a real impetus to spend daily time with God and to document that time by journaling.

Starting A Pursuit Group

Another important development happened after a women's retreat. She and two ladies from her church discussed starting a different kind of group that would encourage their spiritual walk. Other ladies were invited and they ended up with a group of four. The group became intimate quickly. They felt they were consistently seeing God work in their lives. Their practice was to spend time with God daily and journal their experience. Every two weeks they would meet and share what God was showing them.

Ellen's pastor coined the name "pursuit group" and several groups began in the church. Ellen explained the value of such a commitment and group:

> I think it helps me be more aware of what is going on with me. Meeting every two weeks with my pursuit group keeps me processing it. Not just writing it down and forgetting it, but reviewing it – looking back over time, chronicling what is happening - so when the resolution happens, I am better able to recognize it. Getting together is a celebration of God being real in our lives. And it needs to be frequent enough that we can each get through our entries during the time together.

Quiet Time Structure

When asked what form her quiet time usually took, Ellen described:

> I think of my quiet time with God as the start of my time with Him for the day....Usually as I wake up, I try to be aware of God and that He loves me and accepts me. I come out then, get some coffee and my journal, and start seriously to talk. I will write my dreams if any. Or I may jump right into talking with Him. Some mornings I ask him what He wants to talk with me about. While I

don't hear an audible voice, I often put something in quotes. It's my voice in my head, but I know the message is from God.

Sometimes I'll read my Enneagram Thought. (This is a daily email from the Enneagram Institute for her type. It will encourage her to be aware of some aspect of the Type One.) I often read the Jesus Calling devotional to give me a jump start. Sometimes the scriptures in the Jesus Calling are something I want to pay attention to. If it's the first part of the week, I will review the sermon from Sunday. That is a way God speaks to me - through good teaching. Most often my time is spent talking to God, writing that down, and recording His responses.

Sometimes it's meditating about who God is. I sit quietly and let Him take me where He wants to take me. Sometimes I'll capture it later, other time it's too huge. I'll just make a note that I went with Him somewhere today because I know I won't be able to capture it completely in my words. Sometimes He gives me specific tasks or insights for the day. He might give me help to manage a situation or remind me of something I need to do. I jot these notes in a certain section of my journal so I can be sure I follow them.

Scripture is an important source of communicating with God. He often reminds me of scripture or speaks to me personally through passages I am reading. My background is such that I know quite a bit about the Bible and am familiar with scripture, but allowing it to be personal to me and to reveal Jesus to me surpasses just having the information.

Enneagram

When asked asked if the Enneagram helped her spiritual growth, Ellen reflected:

> The Type 1, Reformer, fits me best. It helps me see I have such a desire to be right. As I learned the rigidity part of the One, I didn't want to be that way. It has helped me see the different personalities as different rather than wrong. I need to allow people to be the way they are. This goes with God's sovereignty.

I don't have to control things. If reality is a certain way, I assume God may have it this way for now.

In brief, Ellen is grateful God has initiated and maintained a relationship with her over the years. She feels she has come to know God more intimately. She is more focused on the present and more willing to accept reality as it is, trusting God is sovereign.

Charles's Story

Tall, with blond hair turning to grey, Charles enjoyed a career in engineering. He rose to CEO where he served the last few years before retirement. His strengths included his work ethic, his appreciation for creative design, his integrity, and his ability to communicate well and affirm others. Over the years he grew into the kind of leader whom people trust, respect, and appreciate. In Charles personal life he was devoted to his wife of forty plus years and his three sons who are all married now with families of their own.

Spiritual Background

Charles grew up in a mainline protestant church in the Midwest. He remembered the teachings as good moral lessons, but he never felt a deeper emotional or spiritual connection with God.

When Charles was a married graduate student, his brother, just four years older, contracted skin cancer. He remembered a weekend when his brother drove four hours to share his faith with Charles and his wife. She accepted Christ as her savior, but Charles was hesitant. He recalled his thought that his brother had gone off the deep end because he was over-religious. He didn't see how his brother could be so sure of his salvation. His brother died two years later at twenty-eight.

Accepting Christ

Soon after, Charles and his wife moved to Dallas to begin his career. Now in the heart of the Bible Belt, they attended a Methodist church with a Sunday school class taught by a Dallas Seminary student. They also put their young son in a Lutheran Bible School. One of the school staff visited with them and shared his faith. The bible study and the witness from the Lutheran man, along with thoughts about his brother's faith, finally led Charles to make a personal commitment to Christ.

The Christian Life

Charles' faith was mostly about going to heaven at that stage. He and his wife became faithful church attenders at an independent Bible church. Having an engineering background, Charles said:

> My focus was to read the bible so I would learn how God wanted me to live. I thought of it as an instructional manual on how to live my life wisely so God would bless me and so that I would honor Him.

TWO CRISES

Just a few years into his career, Charles was in charge of a fifty million dollar building project. One of the contractors went bankrupt and as it turned out; his bonding insurance was not active. The client suffered a million dollar loss and sued Charles' company for the money.

> When I found out they were suing us, I was devastated. I remember sitting in my car, leaning over the steering wheel with tears streaming down his cheeks, "I felt like I had done my best...I had done everything right, yet I was sure I would get fired.

Charles recalled thinking: "God you're showing me that You can do whatever you want...even when I do my best, I'm not in control of the outcome." It turned out his company's insurance covered the loss, and his boss was supportive. Charles said, "Because it smoothed over, I went back to my usual behavior of trying to do everything right...acting like I was in control again. I acted as though nothing had happened."

The second major crisis occurred when Charles' second grandson was born. Charles' recalled, "We knew he had Cystic Fibrosis but as it turned out, that was just the beginning. We found he was also autistic with low brain mass and scarring on the brain. He wouldn't eat, and finally had to be fed with a stomach tube. We realized his condition would not get better and that he would probably never be able to live independently on his own."

This hit Charles hard, and he was faced once again with the fact that he was not in control. About this same time Charles' pastor did a series on Joseph and a series on Daniel. The shocking truth was God's sovereignty. He orchestrated huge losses and changes in the lives of these two men to accomplish His will.

> These teachings on top of my grandson's severe disability helped me realize I had lived my life depending on me. And depending on me doing what I thought God wanted. I had read the Bible as an instruction manual. After you've learned to adjust the dials on your stereo, you don't need to keep reading the manual. You think you've got it so why keep reading the manual (Bible). I was living my life morally, but I didn't really have a close relationship with God.

When Charles realized his plans and his efforts were not enough, he saw that he needed to look to God to provide meaning as well. At this point Charles knew he needed to spend daily time with God. "How could I hear God's leading if I never spent time with Him...if I wasn't close to Him?"

New Spiritual Practice

That's when he became drawn to a committed pursuit of God.

> It made me want to be closer to Him and let Him lead. I started reading the Bible as a love letter to me...as a book where Christ reveals Himself to me personally. I committed to spending time with Him almost every day. I read the bible slowly...no certain amount each day...soaking in what is being revealed to me. And I now journal as I read. I write on my computer because I can type fast and I can better record my thoughts. I typically read a section of scripture and type it in my journal as I read. Then I write down the thoughts Christ places in my mind, and then later I might re-write the same section of scripture as though God were saying it to me. All of the writing in my journal is written as a direct conversation between my Heavenly Father and me. I just talk with Him, and I view my entire time as a prayer...as a

conversation with the creator of the Universe. All of this has been revolutionary for me. I began to see that God was intimately involved in my daily life. It wasn't all about me and what I thought...what I planned. God is really there with me! I can't describe the change...it has been so dramatic. It's really like I was once blind, but now I see.

Transformation

After three and a half years of pursuing God in this way, Charles contrasted the majority of his Christian life, with his current experience:

> It makes me tearful that I was so hard-headed. I drove down the highway of life in control...ignoring the huge billboards from God on each side of the road. I was so focused on where I was going and what I thought God wanted me to do that I wasn't taking time to watch and listen to Him for direction. I was self-directed instead of God-led. I had trusted God for salvation but not for my life.

Charles says he still struggles with how to hear God.

> My tendency is to want clear direction, but I think He just wants me to listen to Him and be available. I keep looking for hard answers, but he just wants me to let go and rest in Him.

> It's difficult for me not to drive, but it's been an amazing journey the last three years. Still, I feel I'm just scratching the surface....The pressure is gone to perform and to do it right.

> Instead, I feel a peace because He is in control. The outcome is not up to me. God is doing it. My job is to hang in there with Him. I still must do things as I follow, but I can trust in Him for the results.

Request For a God Weekend

Charles told me the story of how his college roommate called him up a few months ago and asked for what he called a "God weekend." His friend explained that he was doubting religion. Priests were molesting children, and church seemed like "play acting." He and his wife wanted to spend a weekend with Charles and his wife, talking about God and whether or not he was real. The friend was concerned...he told Charles up front that while he would probably not agree with much that would be said...he wanted to leave the weekend with them still friends. With that caveat, they agreed to meet.

Charles said that his inclination was to prepare homework for the weekend and bone up on how to convince his friend about the reality of Christian faith. But talking with God about it, he decided just to show up without a real agenda. Everyone shared two timelines of their life...the first showing key milestones along the way, the second timeline showing God's pursuit...how God had reached out to get their attention through life's circumstances.

Over three or four days, each of the four took turns sharing. Charles and his wife shared their struggles such as their little grandson's many disabilities and how God had shown himself to be real and loving and sufficient through that and other circumstances. Charles was amazed that with almost everything he shared, his friend, the skeptic, was open, accepting, and even appreciative. He struggled with the pressures of trying to be in control...trying to do what was right....trying to be responsible, so hearing God's loving provision in Charles' life encouraged him too. His friend began to see God in a different way and has now begun his own pursuit of God. Charles shared that it was an amazing gift to watch God change a heart right before his eyes. He knew that no words were spoken that were especially persuasive...there was no grand plan to save his friend. He was just privileged to watch God work in another person's life.

Claire's Story

Claire grew up in an Episcopal family. She remembered being at church frequently for the numerous services and events. She recalled always being aware God existed.

> I would ride my bicycle through the neighborhood and talk to God. I don't remember Him ever talking back. In sixth grade I kept a diary and enjoyed writing my private thoughts to God.

Academic performance took priority in Claire's life and she earned the honor of valedictorian in a large public high school. As she prepared her speech, she thought it odd she didn't have anything meaningful to say.

Claire chose University of Texas for college, which represented a big change in her life. It felt scary. At UT everything seemed so open and unstructured. It felt like anything was possible.

Regarding her spiritual journey, Claire related that during college she found a Bible church with incredible teaching. The pastor, a graduate of Dallas Theological Seminary, came from a different theology than her Episcopal background. Claire found herself excited about all the new things she learned about her faith. With some embarrassment, Claire recalled on trips back home she would share with her high school piano teacher/mentor from her church, almost as if to correct the theology she had learned growing up.

From Accounting to Seminary

Claire graduated with an accounting degree from UT and passed her CPA exam the first time. She took a job with an auditing firm in Dallas. It didn't take her long to figure out auditing was not the kind of accounting she enjoyed. Being in Dallas and frustrated with her job, she decided to take advantage of Dallas Seminary. She began a two-year degree in biblical studies.

> I was in my element. I loved studying theology and got by financially working part-time as an accountant. Claire met her future husband at the seminary. Both felt a strong interest in foreign missions. After marriage they lived in Texas and California as they raised support to go to Yugoslavia. Eastern Europe had proven to be a difficult place for American missionaries, but they were idealistic and gung ho for the challenge.

Mission Field

They arrived in Yugoslavia with one son, and their second son was born during their first year on the field. It was exciting and meaningful but by the time of their first furlough, they knew their second son had some serious developmental problems. They returned to the states to have him assessed. They learned he was on the autistic spectrum and needed to be in a one-language country with special schooling. Having to return from the mission field after all the language training and foundational work was confusing and disheartening, but it needed to be done for their son.

Claire's husband heard of a job opportunity in Dallas and Dallas schools had a strong program for autism. So they moved to Dallas. The job possibility fell through, but a position with a missions agency opened. Claire recalls it being an extremely demanding time:

> I had four kids under age six, one of whom was a baby, and one of whom was a special needs child. I would get up at 5 am to get them ready to go to their various schools. And then all the house stuff and cooking and homework, I was exhausted. I reminded God I wanted to be on the mission field, but I was willing to do

this if that's what He wanted. I told Him I could do it if I could make sense of it.

Pastor's Wife

After a couple of years, Claire's husband took the pastorate of a church in North Dallas. The next few years she experienced the stresses of raising four kids, working at the church part-time doing accounting, and teaching a women's bible study. An equal stress was now having a pastor for a husband and all the long hours and criticism he endured. She often felt he had another woman, and it was the church. The year 2007 brought numerous disappointments with people leaving the church and various family stresses. Claire kept going to church and being a mother and wife, but she really distanced herself from God. He had taken away her career dream of being a missionary, and He hadn't helped her make sense of all the stresses

By 2009 her husband was experiencing burnout and the elders recommended he take a six-month sabbatical. She still had all her responsibilities and was burned out herself, but she didn't get a sabbatical. At the end of her husband's sabbatical, they saw a minister/counselor who served burned out clergy. The information she heard about burnout and emotions made sense, but she was too exhausted. She remembers expressing much anger to her husband for not being there for the family because he was working so hard at the church. He acknowledged her feelings and it felt good to unload it, but there was still a lot of hurt and resentment toward God and others.

In the fall of 2010, Claire's husband taught a series on discipleship. He outlined several characteristics of a disciple. Julie said she met most of the characteristics. The one she didn't meet was spending time with Jesus every day. Because of all the stress and disappointments, she just couldn't commit to that daily time with God.

Breakthrough

Early in 2011, Claire and a couple of friends decided to create a group called a Pursuit Group. They would meet every two weeks and share their journal entries on their conversations with God/Jesus. Within a few weeks, the church had the annual Women's Retreat in East Texas. That Friday night one of her best friends mentioned something about the True Self. Claire said in an angry tone, "What does that even mean?" They talked. Her friend told her that there was something blocking her from talking and getting close to God. There was a long, long silence. Finally Claire began to cry. "I wailed." Claire, with the accountant personality, was not one to get emotional, much less wail. Letting her pain out was long overdue. As she went to bed that night, she felt a little better – like a great burden had been lifted off her back.

By the next morning, the resentment was gone. Later that morning the speaker told the story of Jesus healing a woman who had been bent over for eighteen years. Claire realized, "That's me." She began telling the other women what had happened. "I was so excited."

By the next Pursuit Group meeting, Claire had been spending time with God and journaling about it. It had been a very meaningful time and she felt Jesus was speaking to her. Not an audible voice of course, but a voice in her head that sounded more like Claire than Claire.

Very soon after this Claire read the little book The Gift of Being Yourself by David J. Benner. It was about the True Self and Claire realized she needed to discover this True Self rather than trying to keep up a front and be the strong, competent person to all who needed her.

Spiritual Practice

When asked what she does in her quiet time, Claire explained:

> I have my red chair that I call my holy place. I sit there and talk to God about what has been going on. I have also usually been reading something in scripture. After I've poured out my stuff, I usually ask Jesus what He thinks. Then I write down what comes to my mind. A big part of this is that I am journaling it all and then I take it to the support group. I am committed to share it

there, not hide, but share my intimate conversation with Jesus. I'm accountable to being real and honest and fessing up to my thoughts and feelings.

Claire said she is amazed that all this growth of the last three years was nothing she planned or did. She says, "God did it." When asked if the Enneagram had been helpful, Claire explained:

The Enneagram has been big in seeing what I can't hide. On the one hand I want to be authentic, but on the other hand, I'm scared to reveal myself, my feelings and flaws. I've had such a strong False Self of competence and knowledge and success.

Kenny's Story

Kenny ran his fingers through his salt and pepper hair and responded to my questions in a quiet, thoughtful way. He remembered always believing in God. There were pastors on his mom and dad's side. He went through a confirmation class as a teen in the Presbyterian Church, but it had little significance to him.

Married at nineteen, Kenny joined the military. Upon completion of his service, he moved to Texas with his wife and two young children. There they became active in a Presbyterian church. Kenny served as an elder.

> I thought believing in God and going to church regularly was what the Christian faith was all about.

A Life in Crisis

After eighteen years, Kenny's marriage fell apart.

> I had two episodes of adultery and my wife wanted out. I became depressed. Maybe I was already depressed. A couple of years before the marriage ended my dad had committed suicide. I was so angry at him and angry at God. Dad had always been the calming force in our family when there was a crisis. I was angry that when he had his crisis, he couldn't calm himself and choose a better option than suicide.

Kenny's dad left a note to his wife, referring to the biblical parable of the shepherd who left the ninety-nine sheep to look for the one sheep that was lost. He said he hoped Christ would come back after him. A tragic loss for Kenny – the man who'd been his Christian role model.

Accepted and Supported

Kenny went through deep depression because of the loss of his marriage and the loss of his dad. He felt much shame about the adultery. He took advantage of counseling and was eventually referred to a church that had a 12 Step program where he worked on sexual addiction. He felt accepted there despite exposing his sin. Kenny began coming to the church and made close relationships in a men's discipleship group.

He recalled one particular Sunday morning:

> One of the first services I went to was a Body Life service where people stood up and shared. I shared I experienced the trauma of divorce. I started crying right there. David and Rob came up and gave me a hug. I will always remember that day because it opened me up to what a family of Christians can be for each other. I talked about my worst problems and was shown a lot of grace.

A Hard Confession

A couple of years after some healing had taken place, Kenny felt he needed to apologize to his former church where he had been involved for eighteen years. His ex-wife and children no longer attended there. Kenny's current pastor accompanied him to meet with the elders of the church. They supported Kenny in making his confession to the congregation.

> I confessed and apologized for committing adultery. It was very stressful and traumatic, but cleansing for me. It was one of the hardest things I ever had to do. They had been my church family and most were still there.

Kenny's path of recovery involved letting go of the good guy, elder image (perhaps False Self) and exposing his secret inner life. He appropriately did most of this work with other men in a 12-Step group and a men's discipleship group. With this work, a truer self based on humility and reality began to emerge.

Accepting Myself

While Kenny believes God was always active in his life, he admits he wasn't aware of it. He feels God allowed him to go through the divorce and tragic loss of his dad to help him come to terms with his sexual issues and emotional issues.

> I had never had a positive view of myself or accepted myself. I didn't have a big ego because I had never been a jock or a good student. I did just enough to pass. I never had the confidence to believe I could do anything well. Realizing that God accepts me, despite what I think of myself or what others think, has been critical for how I feel about myself today.

One of the powerful experiences that helped Kenny see how God felt about him happened when his church had the author, Brennan Manning, speak at the men's retreat:

> Manning talked about the prodigal son and how the father saw his son at a distance returning. He ran to his son and kissed him and welcomed him. It didn't matter what he'd done. He didn't even ask what he'd done. The father celebrated his return. It helped me see that God had never turned away from me. I had turned away and He waited for me to come back.

While Kenny has not taken the Enneagram, he has taken the Myers-Briggs. He is an ISFP (introvert, sensing, feeling, perceiving). It helped him understand how he was different than other men. He was more sensitive and gentle. It also explained why he values relationships so much. He observed that he is often the one initiating and keeping up relationships in his family and at church. He feels this is one of the ways he is like his Dad.

Learning to Trust

Kenny said he now sees God as interactive:

> It's a relationship where he wants me to trust Him. Our pastor has been teaching about the Israelites coming out of Egypt and their experience in the wilderness. God wanted them to trust Him. And it's the same with me. I resort to sin at times because I don't believe God will meet my needs. I don't really trust him. At

times when I do trust Him. I pray and ask for His help and I feel victory.

The recent challenge for Kenny has been the loss of his job and trusting God to help him find another one. Through the contact of one of the men in his old discipleship group, God gave him a great job with more pay and lots more responsibility.

I don't think I'm competent enough for this job, but God tells me to lean on Him and trust Him. While I don't read my Bible and pray and journal every morning, I am very cognizant throughout the day that I need God's help if this is going to work. He got me the job and if I can keep the job, it is only because He is helping me.

Teresa's Story

Background

Teresa, a petite brunette with a warm smile, grew up in a conservative Christian home. She had two younger brothers and was close to them. Her father was a quiet, intellectual person who affirmed and enjoyed her and let her tag along. The relationship with her mother was more strained at times. Teresa would try to please her but often felt criticized. "She encouraged me to dress up pretty and look good while she criticized her own appearance, even though she is beautiful."

Motherhood

Motherhood eventually gave Teresa a deep sense of worth.

> Children gave me purpose and started to give me a picture of what unconditional love looks/feels like. They were mine, and in some sense, I felt the first good thing I had ever done. I felt like being a mom came naturally and I poured my soul into it. I provided for them, I nurtured them, I played with them, I took them everywhere with me, I read to them, I took them to church, I sang to them and I kissed them when they were sad or hurt.

During these years, Teresa took charge of life and felt in control of her circumstances and future. She determined to be happy, to be a good mother and a good wife, and to keep her house well. She decided,

> I will keep everyone happy and no one will ever want for more. I've got this. I know how to take care of those I love and I know how to be nice about it.

Crisis

However, in my early to mid-thirties, the illusion of this thinking began to crumble. For years I had kept a full-time job as an accountant working from home and taking care of my two babies. During this time my husband worked in consulting and traveled a lot. This was hard and I often felt lonely. The summer before my oldest was to start school, we decided to move to Dallas since my job had an office there and my husband could take a sales position with that company.

But things took a down turn and with a house purchased based on their old income level, Teresa's family found themselves spending more than they made. They were being swallowed up in credit card debt and stress. Although Teresa watched every penny, they kept losing ground.

Teresa realized,

> I had for years tried to alter my behavior and thinking to convince myself that I was in fact good and worthy of love. What I didn't want to admit was that my flawed thinking and self-pride had told me I could just focus my "can do" attitude toward positive, worthwhile living, and I would succeed in having a good, worthwhile, happy life. My pursuit of happiness was still high on my list of what a "successful, fulfilled life looks and feels like."

> I broke. I was exhausted. I wanted a way out. I knew I was failing at trying to keep things together. I was ashamed of my choices and thoughts. I was ashamed of where we were and how I had failed to do a better job. At the end of myself, I cried out to God. I literally fell on my knees and cried out to Him. I told him of my sorrow and I cried for help. I told him I was sorry and that I was a failure and I needed him.

At this point, Teresa realized she didn't know God, but rather she knew about him. And yet she had asked him for help.

> In his faithfulness, Jesus showed up. He put a desire in my heart to get to know him. I began to talk to him regularly and I had a deep desire to follow him, rather than my own flawed thinking.

Confession

Teresa revealed her personal story contained a lot of fear, doubt, regret, and shame.

> I needed to talk to God about these. I needed to be open and honest with him about things he already knew and then let him heal and redeem me. I didn't really do anything but come to him, talk to him, listen, and then do what he asked me to do. I did have to choose to be obedient. It was a process, and still is, and is something I will be working on with God the rest of my life.

Pursuing God

Although Teresa had tried quiet-time devotions, trying to connect with God through using a devotion book or Bible study, she couldn't stick with it and it didn't connect her to God. Yet now she found herself in a place in life where her sense of control was challenged.

> My life philosophy was if you try hard enough, if you put your mind to it, you can do anything. That was being challenged in a big way and I was failing.
>
> What I began to see and feel and hear God continually saying to me was one simple phrase, "Let me do it. Let me change you." All I did was have a deep longing desire to grow my relationship with God. I wanted to let God be in charge of me. So I started praying...even at times crying out for God to help me.

All of this Teresa chronicled in her journal. Her times of crying out became honest interchanges with God in which she bared her soul and he gave her truth.

Teresa also realized that she could no longer "work" for her redemption. She had to lay down her self-pride, "can do good" attitude at Jesus' feet admitting that only Jesus redeems and transforms.

Next came confessions from her youth. Rocky parts of her teen and young adult years revealed a longing to be good, but rebellious behavior instead. "I knew this about myself, but I had never been able to truly look at it and feel it without running from the pain that was hidden and buried deep behind closed doors.

Teresa recalled that more memories and confessions followed for the next days. "I came to an overwhelmingly deep realization of how Jesus had pursued me across all those years, through all that rebellion. My rebellion wasn't bigger than his love for me."

Her confessions brought healing. Even now, over two years later, it brings a flood of tears. "Jesus was helping me know myself more so I would know him more and trust him more. He loves me, not who I think I need to be. Isn't Jesus sweet!"

Scripture

Regarding the use of the Bible, Teresa shared:

> In my experience being able to connect with God's word came once I "got real" with Jesus. I didn't hold back my thoughts and emotions in fear that Jesus would reject me or forsake me. I had to give all to Him, in faith, not knowing for sure what would happen. When I did, it opened up a dialogue and new eyes to His Word. His Word then became living in my heart. When I read his words and message he was speaking directly to me jumped off the pages. I began to long for time to just sit and read and hear his voice speak to me in the pages of scripture.
>
> I had grown up reading the Bible and/or doing devotions from time to time because it was the right thing to do. But now that God and I were talking on a regular basis, I knew I could trust him. I knew that he loved me no matter what. It opened up a whole new world of discovering what the scriptures have to say. What they have to say specifically to me.

Teresa advises about reading God's word:

> Slow down! Take the time necessary to understand the words, picture the story and all that is happening in your mind. Then read it again. I like to read and write down in my journal what comes to mind. Sometimes it's a summary of the story; sometimes it's a specific aspect of the passage that jumps out at me. Then spend some time exploring what you have written. Journal all your thoughts. I have found that the truth God wants to reveal to me comes not from the immediate reading, but rather from deeper pondering. Jesus has taught me to sit still, quiet my

mind, and listen for his still small voice. His gentle truth comes as a whisper, but grips my heart and soul in a way that lets me know it is Him with me and in me.

Enneagram

The Enneagram has been helpful to Teresa's increasing awareness of herself, her reactions and her interactions with others. "It opened up a reality bigger than myself. It also gave me a sense of relief: it's ok that I am this way. I was made this way."

Type 2 of the Enneagram fit for Teresa. She had tried to earn love: the need to put other people's needs ahead of her own; to give in order to get; to earn a place in the affections of others because love will not simply be given.

I experienced a sense of clarity about my own reactions and decisions. I started to more clearly see myself as I really am, and honestly, I didn't quite like what I saw.

I started to have feelings I didn't understand. I questioned about myself, 'Who is this person?' It was hard to stay present to some of the feelings that arose in me.

The honest truth about my ego dependence was shocking to say the least. It was painful. I knew I had to let it go, but it was all I had ever known. It was scary. I learned what faith and hope really are."

Helpful Books

Teresa mentioned several books she read that confirmed she was on the right track seeking Jesus. Before Jesus led me to read about the Enneagram, he had me reading a book called *The Gift of Being Yourself.* I believe Jesus used this book and our personal conversations to prepare me for the way he would use the Enneagram to make me more aware of myself and the defenses I had adopted to protect my heart from more wounding." Other books God provided along the way were *When the Heart Waits* and *He Calls Me Beloved.* These books made serious contributions to Teresa's honest pursuit of relationship with God often describing life events and conversations with God amazingly similar to her own.

Since Teresa has always loved music and been influenced by it, she uses music as a way to connect to God. She downloads worship songs, particularly those that are scripture in song, then spends time alone listening and praying those words back to God. Journaling her thoughts about the songs are helpful. "Don't edit. Don't be afraid to write exactly what comes to mind. God did start speaking to me, not audibly, but in my mind."

Over the years Teresa has chronicled the journey of a deepening relationship with Jesus. She knows herself much better and she knows Jesus much better. However, she has no illusions about this being a finished process. She knows this will be a life-long process, an eternal process, but she is assured of her relationship with Jesus because of the history they have shared,

> I am remembering what Jesus told me a few weeks back when he was showing me more about myself. I confessed to him that I was feeling worthless and realizing it was because I wasn't getting the reaction and response from others that I thought I wanted/needed. In that moment of confession, "I feel worthless Jesus," Jesus softly answered, "I give you your worth, Teresa, don't doubt My worth." I cried to Jesus, apologizing for my lack of faith, for my lack of worship in who he is and what his worth means for me. His worth means everything to me.

Ben's Story

Ben, raised in a conservative, Presbyterian family, always went to church. He accepted Christ into his heart when he was nine. He didn't feel much was different other than he felt sure about going to heaven. In high school, he remembered balking at going to church. His parents' responded by requiring more church involvement. He felt oppressed.

At university, Ben studied electrical engineering. During these years he didn't have to go to church so he didn't. Ben recalled:

> Toward the end of college, I started to wonder if there was something about God that could make a difference in my life. Up until then I had felt Christian music was bad and Christian women were boring. I didn't see God as being able to provide the things I wanted.

Discussions with two Christian friends gradually helped him see that God could provide his needs:

> As a senior I accepted Christ again. This time I really knew what I was getting into. After college, I attended bible studies and went to men's groups, but I really didn't feel I was drawing close to God.

Turning Points: Food and Money

Four years ago, Ben faced the fact he was sixty pounds overweight. He knew he needed to change his approach to food and that he needed structure. Ben made a decision and commitment. He began Weight Watchers. He tracked everything he ate and stayed with their point system. It worked. He lost sixty pounds.

A year later, he realized he and his wife had too much debt and always struggled financially. He decided to study Dave Ramsey's material from Financial Peace University. They followed his recommendations closely and it worked. They got their debt under control and lived within their budget.

Ben said these two successes amazed him. Both changes came about with an intentional pursuit.

My pastor had been encouraging us to spend time with God. He invited me to attend a weekly pursuit group with a few men. We each committed to spending time with God, talking and listening. We would journal and meet once a week to discuss our relationship with Christ.

Ben explained that this intentional pursuit of God has helped him experience God as much more personal. He said,

> It's like if I heard President Obama on TV ask people to donate to a good cause. I might consider it, but I'd probably not get around to doing it. But if the President knocked on my door and asked me to donate, I would probably do what he asked."

Previous View of God

When asked how he saw God before this intentional pursuit, Ben said,

> I believed He created everything and started it off – like a top and gave it a spin. All the planets, everything. He's sitting up there waiting for us to die. (Laugh) Now I realize God is revealing Himself in everything, whether we see it or not. It is a matter of Him opening our eyes to it.

Daily Spiritual Practice

When asked how he spends his intentional pursuit time, Ben described:

> Most every day I try to spend time in God's word by myself. Usually the kids are getting ready for school and I put in my earplugs. I spend thirty minutes to one hour writing to God what is on my mind and reading His word. Then I write back what I think He is saying to me through the passage. "What is He saying about Himself, and what is He saying to me?"

Sometimes I start "Dear Ben," then write what I think God would say. I'll embellish it with things I think God might be bringing in from the passage. Things come to my mind. A lot of time in that process, I really hear what God wanted to say. Because it is something I needed to hear. It addresses my problem.

God Confronts

Many times God encourages me and affirms His love for me. At other times He confronts.

Ben once told his wife he had strong feelings about controlling illegal immigration. Some months later in one of his quiet times, he read a scripture where God instructed the Israelites to let the foreigners in to be a part of their country. God said that this is His kingdom, His land, and He wanted to share it with foreigners.

> God changed my stance. I had looked at it like this is my country and we have to defend it against illegal aliens. I didn't bring this issue up to God, but He brought it up to me through His word.

Ben reported another time he was reading in Ezekiel about the valley of dry bones. God said He would raise up dry bones and ligaments and form a vast army.

> I realized what God had been doing in me. I was dry bones. My flesh had fallen off. I was spiritually dead. I didn't even realize how desperate it was until God told me. He is restoring me.

Epilogue

Three years ago, I struggled with how to write about Knowing Yourself and Knowing God. At some point I was reminded that stories are more readable than textbooks. Thus, I began to recall and record my journey to know myself.

My most important insights while writing this book have been:

- Since my ego is limited, it shouldn't be automatically running my life.

- The more I am aware of my ego strivings, the better I can distinguish "my way" from "God's way."

- My surest sense of identity, is that I am a beloved child of God.

- As I grow in a more intimate relationship with God, I live more peacefully in the moment, available to join in what He is doing.

My hope is that through your study of this book, you have a general blueprint for Knowing Yourself and Knowing God:

- Face and process your psychological wounds and feelings.

- Know your Myers-Briggs and Enneagram types.

- Share deeply with Christian friends, supporting and challenging one another to growth.

- Make time to pursue God; listen to what He has for you.

What's Next for Me?

Four tasks are in my plans:

- Explore ways to make this book available to those who might find it helpful.

- Continue to work in my psychology practice, but learn to do it less in my strength and more in His strength.

- Put the finishing touches on my treehouse. I look forward to getting back to the silence of the woods, and working with my hands once again.

- Spend time with my grandchildren – a boy and three little girls!

I put these four things on paper to distinguish these as "my plans." While I intend to invest my time in these worthy endeavors, I will try to be open to redirection from God. For how can I really know in advance what God has next for me? I don't think I'm meant to know. I'm just supposed to spend time with Him and follow any direction He may give.

I am intrigued by His power and desire to transform His children. What if He helped me be more free of my INFP personality type and my Enneagram, Type 4? What if I weren't so timid and introverted? What if I weren't so in need of others' approval? What if I really trusted God to provide for me financially? What if I became free to live in the moment and discern and follow the adventure He lays before me?

In closing, I feel very grateful for this opportunity to share my story with you. It hasn't always been easy, but I see God has taken me to where I needed to be. If what I have shared helps you, then I am thrilled and honored. May you find your True Self in God.

* * * * * *

You may follow and connect with John Shackelford through www.KnowingYourselfKnowingGod.com

Appendix

Important Ego Functions

Reality Testing:	It helps me distinguish between what is going on in my mind from what is going on in outside reality. Example: I have an argument with my spouse at breakfast. When at work, the boss doesn't smile when she sees me. I'm sure she is mad at me. This is poor reality testing. If I had better reality testing, I might think, "The boss didn't smile this morning. I wonder what's going on with her?" I would be able to distinguish my frustration with my spouse from the behavior of my boss.
Impulse Control:	The ego helps me slow down an impulse rather than expressing it immediately. Example: A car pulls out right in front of me so that I have to brake hard to avoid hitting it. I quickly shoot the driver some sign language I learned in junior high. This is poor impulse control. If I had good impulse control, I would feel the anger but be able to engage my thinking. "That guy could be unstable. He could become aggressive. I'll just let it go."
Regulation of Feelings:	The ego helps me control my feelings when I need to. Example: During a meeting at work, I receive some harsh criticism. I burst into tears. If I have better regulation of feelings, I delay crying and maintain a more professional demeanor. If I need to cry, I'll do so later in the restroom or in my car.
Judgment:	The ego helps me make good decisions. Example: While on a business trip, an attractive work colleague invites me to stop by their room for a drink. I might want to say "Yes," but with better judgment, I say, "I'm really tired. I just need some time to myself."
Good Relationships:	The ego helps me make and maintain healthy relationships that meet my social and intimacy needs. Example: As a college freshmen, I meet these cool guys who like to party and very seldom study. I'm spending more and more time with them. My main priority is doing well in school, so I seek new friends, who also spend the necessary time studying.
Thought Processes:	My ego helps organize my thoughts so that I can gather information and think logically, sensibly, and make good decisions. Example: Fearing I may have made a major mistake at work, I consider quitting

	since I'll probably get fired anyway. My ego puts on the brakes (impulse control) and I consider other options. I realize that I messed up at work but know that I can learn from this mistake and do better next time. I talk with my supervisor about it and look for ways to avoid this in the future.
Defensive Functioning:	The ego helps me avoid debilitating anxiety. I can put worries and emotional issues in the background while I deal with my present responsibilities. Example: I checked my bank balance this morning and I'm overdrawn with $140 lost in overdraft fees. At work I can't stop thinking about this and beating myself up. My healthy ego realizes I'm overdrawn and will have to pay the penalties. If I have some money, I will deposit it and try to be more careful next time. I repress this frustration and am able to give all my focus to my work.

(Freud, The Ego and the Id (The Standard Edition of the Complete Psychological Works of Sigmund Freud), 1990)

References

Adamson, A. (Director). (2005). *The Chronicles of Naria: The Lion, the Witch, and the Wardrobe* [Motion Picture].

Benner, D. (2011). *Soulful Spirituality*. Grand Rapids: Baker Publishing Group.

Benner, D. G. (2004). *The Gift of Being Yourself*. Downers Grove, ILL: Inter-Varsity.

Berkof, L. (1959). *Systematic Theology*. Banner of Truth.

Bowen, M. (1985). *Family Therapy in Family Practice*. Rowan and Littlefield Publishers, Inc.

Freud, S. (1990). *The Ego and the Id (The Standard Edition of the Complete Psychological Works of Sigmund Freud*. W.W. Norton & Company.

Freud, S. (1990). *The Ego and the Id (The Standard Edition of the Complete Psychological Works of Sigmund Freud)*. W. W. Norton & Company.

Freud, S. (2001). *The Complete Psychological Works of Sigmund Freud: " The Ego and the Id " and Other Works v. 19*. Vintage.

Freud, S. (2001). *The Complete Psychological Works of Sigmund Freud: "The Ego and the ID" and Other Works V. 19*. Vintage.

Gilquist, P. (1970). *Love Is Now*. Grand Rapids, MI: Zondervan Publishing House.

Gladwell, M. (2012). *Outliers*. Hatchett Book Group Inc.

Harris, T. (1967). *I'm OK - You're OK.* New York: Harper and Row.

Hooper, T. (Director). (2012). *Les Miserables* [Motion Picture].

Joines, V. a. (2012). *TA Today: An Introduction to Transactional Analysis.* On Amazon.

Jung, C. a. (1976). *The Portable Jung.* New York: Penguin.

Keirsey, D. &. (1984). *Please Understand Me: Character and Temperment Types.* Prometheus Nemesis Book Company.

Keirsey, D. (1998). *Please Understand Me II: Temperament, Character, Intelligence.* Prometheus Nemesis Book Company.

Keirsey, D. (1998). *Please Understand Me: Temperment, Character, Intelligence.* Prometheus Nemesis Book Company.

Keirsey, D., & Bates, M. (1984). *Please Understand Me: Character and Temperament Types.* Prometheus Nemesis Book Company.

Kidd, S. (2006). *When the Heart Waits: Spiritual Direction for Life's Sacred Questions.* Harper One.

Kidd, S. M. (2006). *When the Heart Waits: Spiritual Direction for Life's Sacred Questions.* HarperOne.

Kroeger, O. a. (1988). *Type Talk.* New York: A Dell Book.

Lord, P. (1988). *Hearing God.* Grand Rapids, MI: Baker Publishing Group.

Lowen, A. (2012). *Narcissism: Denial of the True Self.* Simon and Schuster.

MacDonald, G. (1997). *When Men Think Private Thoughts.* Nashville, Tn: Thomas Nelson.

Manning, B. (2002). *Abba's Child: The Cry of the Heart for Intimate*

Belonging. NavPress.

Manning, B. (2002). *Abba's Child: The Cry of the Heart for Intimate Belonging.* Nav Press.

Miller, K. (1997). *The Secret Life of the Soul.* Broadman & Holman Publishing.

Moon, G. (2009). *Falling for God.* Waterbrook Press.

Ortberg, J. (2002). *The Life You've Always Wanted.* Grand Rapids, MI: Zondervan.

Palmer, H. (1991). *The Enneagram: Understanding Yourself and the Others in Your Life.* San Francisco: Harper.

Riso, D. a. (1996). *Personality Types.* New York: Houghton Mifflin Company.

Riso, D. a. (1999). *The Wisdom of the Enneagram.* New York: Bantum Books.

Riso, D. a. (2000). *Understanding the Enneagram.* New York: Houghton Mifflin Company.

Rohr, R. (2011). *The Enneagram: A Christian Perspective.* New York: The Crossland Publishing Company.

Sproul, R. (1012). *Who Is the Holy Spirit?* Reformation Trust Publishing.

Stewart, I. a. (2012). *TA Today: A New Introduction to Transactional Analysis.* On Amazon.

Swindoll, C. (2013). *www.insight.org/broadcast/library.* Retrieved from www.insight.org: http://www.insight.org/store/monthly-resources/guilt-grace-and-gratitude-dst.html

Whitfield, C. (1987). *Healing the Child Within.* Deerfield Beach, FL:

Healthy Communicatins, Inc.

Young, S. (2004). *Jesus Calling*. Nashville, TN: Thomas Nelson.

Made in the USA
San Bernardino, CA
01 February 2016